COURAGE TO Create

"With personable, conversational prose, Clare McCallan lays out a vision of hope for the Catholic artist. The mixture of vividly portrayed personal anecdotes and prayerful reflection assures us that a life dedicated to God through the creative process is indeed possible. McCallan invites all of us to be cocreators with God, the Master Artist."

Emily Claire Schmitt
Executive director of Catholic Artist Connection

"If you have ever wondered what your creative gifts might be and whether or not you should bother to explore them at all, this piece will charge and implore you to do so. Clare McCallan's faith-driven narrative will show you how necessary it is to be, share, and embrace who you are and what you can do to bring light, love, and hope to our world."

Gracie Morbitzer
Artist of The Modern Saints

"In a world where success in art is often quantified by production and results, McCallan does an excellent job of bringing artists back to the true source of creativity, God himself. I was particularly moved by McCallan's assessment of how suffering and woundedness become sources of creativity for an artist when understood in light of the Cross of Christ."

JohnMarc Skoch
Singer, songwriter, and FOCUS music director

"There is nothing more powerful than a testimony. I was moved and inspired by McCallan's vulnerability and reminded that there are no 'small talents' in God's Kingdom. All we need to do is to trust God to work through our finiteness. As a singer and songwriter, I have seen how lives can be transformed through the beauty of music. I encourage you to read this book and discover within yourself gifts that God can use in a powerful way, if you will only let him."

Fr. Rob Galea
Singer, songwriter, and author

Unleashing Your Artistic Gifts

FOR TRUTH, BEAUTY, AND GOODNESS

COURAGE TO *Create*

CLARE McCALLAN

FOREWORD BY VALERIE DELGADO

Ave Maria Press　AVE　Notre Dame, Indiana

Scripture quotations are from *New Revised Standard Version Bible*, copyright © 1989 National Council of the Churches of Christ in the United States of America. Used by permission. All rights reserved.

Foreword © 2023 by Valerie Delgado

© 2024 by Clare McCallan

All rights reserved. No part of this book may be used or reproduced in any manner whatsoever, except in the case of reprints in the context of reviews, without written permission from Ave Maria Press®, Inc., P.O. Box 428, Notre Dame, IN 46556, 1-800-282-1865.

Founded in 1865, Ave Maria Press is a ministry of the United States Province of Holy Cross.

www.avemariapress.com

Paperback: ISBN-13 978-1-64680-287-6

E-book: ISBN-13 978-1-64680-288-3

Cover image © gettyimages.com.

Cover and text design by Katherine Robinson.

Printed and bound in the United States of America.

Library of Congress Cataloging-in-Publication Data is available.

CONTENTS

Foreword	BY VALERIE DELGADO	VII
Introduction	LET'S GET CREATIVE!	XI
Chapter 1	A PLACE TO CALL HOME	1
Chapter 2	WHAT MAKES AN ARTIST?	13
Chapter 3	HOW TO MAKE IT LOOK AS IF YOU'RE HAVING FUN DANCING	27
Chapter 4	FEED THE HUNGER INSIDE YOU	43
Chapter 5	MAKING SPACE	57
Chapter 6	SUCCESS IS THE BEST REVENGE	75
Chapter 7	CREATING WITH YOUR CROSS	91
Chapter 8	LABOR TOWARD NEW LIFE	103
Chapter 9	THEATER KIDS WILL INHERIT THE WORLD	117
Conclusion	TELL ME ABOUT THE VIEW . . .	127
Appendix	YOUR "ARTIST DATES"	133
Notes		144

Foreword

Being a Catholic creative is a profound calling that marries the sacred and the artistic. It is a journey filled with moments of introspection and awe, and an unwavering commitment to channeling divine inspiration onto whatever your "canvas" might be. Within this call, the act of creation becomes an act of worship; each stroke of the brush, pen, word, or dance, an offering of devotion.

I first felt this calling when I was twenty years old and feeling so lost. I had just completed another year of community college and started working part time at my local parish as I tried to figure out what I wanted to do with my life. Thinking about the future paralyzed me. Here I was, still enrolled in college (because that is what is expected) while very much not wanting to go to school. I prayed about this . . . a lot. And every time, all I *thought* I heard was crickets. But one day after leaving work, I had this deep urge to stop by my local craft store and buy some paint. I don't fully know how to describe it other than there was this creative thirst inside of me that needed to be quenched. So, I bought a bunch of paint supplies, brought them home, and just started painting. Canvas after canvas, I painted as if I were running out of time.

What did I paint? My prayers. It was as if for the first time, my mind was clear, my worries weren't so big anymore, and my prayers were left on a canvas for the Lord to see. With every stroke of the brush, I felt myself drawing closer to something beyond the physical realm—an ethereal connection to the divine. As I poured my emotions onto the canvas and channeled my thoughts through my brush, I sensed an unfolding dialogue with God.

I left school that year and, a few years later, decided to quit my job to pursue art full time. The decision to step away from the traditional path of going to college and embrace a life devoted to creating art was not one made lightly. Did my parents approve? Absolutely not. Questions of "How will you provide for yourself?"; "How will you afford health insurance?"; and "What's your plan if this doesn't work out?" followed me at every turn. What I realized is that at the end of the day, despite seeing some validity to their concern, their questions didn't matter. Don't get me wrong—I love my parents. But this was between me and God. In leaving behind the familiar, I embarked on a pilgrimage of creativity and devotion to all that is true, good, and beautiful. This shift meant embracing uncertainty and risk, but also unlocking a profound sense of purpose and alignment. Each picture drawn and canvas painted became a testament to my commitment to creating with and for the Creator of the universe.

Throughout these pages, you will encounter stories from Clare and others who embraced their identity as artists. They faced skepticism, navigated the labyrinth of self-doubt, and stared down the abyss of the unknown. Yet they persevered. They found those moments of creative communion, where they not only cultivated their artistic abilities but also nurtured a profound relationship with God, finding solace, guidance, and a deeper understanding of the world. We all need a creative community where our hearts ignite with inspiration as we work together to bring truth, beauty, and goodness into the world.

Foreword

This book is a beautiful reminder of these three great transcendentals and a wonderful resource for anyone wanting to take that leap to become an artist. As you begin this book, take a moment to reflect on and embrace your own artistic journey. Use the "Artist Moments" sections to create something beautiful. Allow your creative spirit to paint stories, sketch emotions, and write words that resonate with the core of your being. Allow this book to inspire, heal, and connect you with the ultimate Creator. In this book, may you find inspiration to follow the unique cadence of your heart.

Valerie Delgado

Introduction

LET'S GET CREATIVE!

When considering who I wrote this book for, I can't help but think about a series of embarrassing videos that I've secretly been recording for just shy of a decade now. No one else knows about these videos (until now), but since I already feel a sort of kinship with you, dear reader, I'll admit it: for the last seven years, I've been recording all of what I thought would be the "big" moments of my journey as an artist but that always ended up being just another rejection letter or empty auditorium.

Invariably I shoot these videos right before heading out to what I believe to be this "life-changing" event, in the slanting bathroom of whatever odd little hole I've decided to slap a mailbox on and call home. And the videos usually feature a crying girl who really, truly, believes that today is her big day.

We don't have to tell her, friend, but it never turns out to be her "big day." Very often, it doesn't even turn out to be a "good day": the meeting she skips her own birthday to take or the grant application she so desperately wants to perfect that she never even sends it in are never marks of a "big day," let alone a "good day."

Not that those moments don't have their merits! The soul-crushing disappointments are outweighed only by the private embarrassment as she returns home and deletes yet another video off her phone.

These moments also have merit as she pulls out her journal and writes a few lines of poetry to work through the pain. And in those little moments, though she'll never realize it (let alone take some self-indulgent video of it), she is having her big break.

A big break from her expectations.

A big break from her twisted idea of vocation.

A big break that creates a crack just wide enough to peek into, to see what type of artist she is capable of becoming.

I'm hoping that this book will prove to be the "big break" you needed in that sense—that it will give you a peek into the possibilities God might have had in mind when he entrusted to you these creative *abilities* and *sensibilities*—however you choose to use them. I originally wrote this book as much for myself—that hapless girl with the video camera—to knock her in the head and bring her to her senses. But I'm also hoping and praying that it speaks to many others just like her.

This is the book I needed when I started as a young Catholic artist in a world that seems increasingly disinterested in truth, beauty, and goodness, favoring instead viral potential, cheap entertainment, and shock factor. And if I needed to read something like this at twenty-two, it would be fair to say that I needed to write something like this at thirty.

My "big moments" look a little different these days. I created and run a Catholic artists' home that has housed over forty people in the last two years. I wrapped on my own TV show a few weeks ago, and I just recently started

Introduction xiii

interviewing Academy Award–winning actors and directors. In a few weeks, I'll travel to cover the Venice Film Festival for the first time. All my dreams are coming true, and yet writing this book reminded me that my "big moments" continue to be my quiet ones. The best poems I write are prayers in the margins of my church's bulletin, and my most important interview subjects are my artist friends, sitting around our kitchen table on a Tuesday morning, laughingly telling me a little bit more about the first time they realized that they really, really loved to sing.

The most centering part of writing this book was interviewing a few of those artist friends to round out each chapter. In these pages, I've included conversations with some of the most talented artists I know, of all ages and stages and mediums. Many of them have lived in my home with me, and more than a few of them have let me stay and create with them over the years. The greatest gift I can give you, reader, is to share my community with you because they are the best part of me and my practice. So please, cherish their words as I do.

So . . . what's the best way to use this book? Perhaps the best way is to go through it with your own community. Interspersed throughout these chapters, you'll find "Artist Moments" features, which are meant to provide you with opportunities to write and draw reflections of your own journey as a creative. Get as creative as you can with these spaces. Write songs and poems, draw portraits, and pull out your watercolors if you have to. I included these blank pages not simply to give you permission to create but in an earnest plea: *Please, please make something beautiful.*

At the end of each chapter, you'll find reflection questions that are perfect for heart-to-hearts over a cup of coffee or a sheet of watercolor paper. These questions are meant to provide moments of creative introspection and are perfect for conversations with friends, classmates, co-creators, or fellow parishioners. As you'll read in these pages, community has been the foundation of my artistic practice, and I believe that if you build yours on the same bedrock, you will find your creativity becomes synonymous with kingdom building.

It was such a joy to create this book for you. The many hours spent hunched over my laptop, in museums and coffee shops and public libraries, were some of the biggest small moments of my life. In the quiet tedium, I reconnected with my Creator and the purpose he has given me in a way that feels a whole lot like that long-awaited "big break." So thank you, dear reader, for giving this to me.

Chapter 1

A PLACE TO CALL HOME

(The Story of St. Joseph's Home for Artisans)

> To criticize, to destroy, is not difficult; any unskilled laborer knows how to drive his pick into the noble and finely hewn stone of a cathedral. To construct: that is what requires the skill of a master.
>
> —St. Josemaría Escrivá

"One . . . two . . . three . . . pull!"

With a herculean effort, Ena, Fernando, and I threw the full force of our collective energies into eradicating the ugly striped wallpaper, ripping it off the wall and casting it onto our floor. As the last of it came free, we squealed with excitement, giving each other a congratulatory hug. Suddenly Ena's voice broke the celebration though:

"Wait, you guys. What is *that*?"

I followed her outstretched arm to the wall. To my horror, the seventies striped wallpaper had been hiding something infinitely worse: streaks of black mold seemed to form an evil, dripping smiley face on our living room wall, mocking us (and our home improvement efforts) gleefully.

My hand flew to my mouth, half in shock and half in an attempt to protect myself from the toxins. We ran out of the building, got in the car, and headed out to buy mold remover and masks, unaware that from that day on, our life would become measurable not only in sweet memories and shared laughs but also in Home Depot visits.

Just three weeks earlier, in the winter of 2020, our parish priest, Fr. Michael, had given us permission to begin restoration of the church's old convent. Fr. Michael told us that if we could clean out and fix up the building, we could use it for our proposed project: to create a home for young Catholic artists to live and grow in their faith and artistry in community. Thrilled, we gratefully accepted, sight unseen. A few days later, Fr. Mike gave us a tour of the old convent we hoped to someday call home.

The phrase "love at first sight" falls short of how we actually felt upon first seeing our home. Our love was sweeter than that and, honestly, dumber than that. Our affections were gleeful, wholeheartedly genuine, and totally nonsensical. So, while "love at first sight" may be too serious and grown-up to describe our doe-eyed affection, "puppy love" fits quite perfectly. We had all the marks of the young and infatuated: in every flaw, we saw a beauty mark; every safety hazard, a charming quirk.

As we were given the first tour of what would become our home, we took turns posing with all the oddities of this delightfully decrepit Boston building—the linoleum living room floors, the seven cramped bedrooms without a single closet (because why would the nuns have needed closets?), and so on. And then Father brought us to the building's greatest—and perhaps only—strength: its rooftop.

On top of one of the most broken-down buildings in Boston lay one of the most expansive rooftops in the city. It had a view of the ocean *and* a view of the city skyline, which is just about impossible for a group of starving artists to find in any city, let alone afford. Jumping up and down, five floors above the bustling streets and five million miles out of our minds, we started shouting out all the ideas we had for hosting open mic nights and dinner parties here atop our new, beautiful, broken home.

"We could have concerts up here! This corner could be the stage so the whole skyline would be behind them!"

"Think about all the dinners we could have up here! We could invite our neighbors. I wonder what they'll be like?"

"What if we put string lights there? And there? Over there and there and there?"

With time, all of those ideas would come to fruition, but first we had to create not only a home that people might want to live in but also a mission that they could get behind. Names for our new home were proposed and argued on, but in the end, it was agreed that as artisans, we should dedicate our home, in the year of St. Joseph, to the patron saint of craftsmen himself.

And thus, "St. Joseph's Home for Artisans" was born.

From March until June, we spent every day scraping wallpaper, treating mold, and painting walls. Quietly, we agreed it wouldn't surprise us if the mold took a few years off our lives. Loudly, as if to show bad luck we weren't scared of it, we proclaimed that that was a risk we were willing to take. We styled each bedroom with the latest and greatest from the Goodwill bargain bin and furnished them with whatever our wealthier neighbors left out for the garbage trucks. As the Dr. Frankensteins of home decor, we shoved together mismatched pieces to create comfortable spaces. By the end though, our home had a unique sort of flair, embodying a style that has since been described as "grandma chic."

Artist Moments

Use this space to sketch out what your dream artist's space would be like. Is it spacious or cozy? What kinds of resources does it have? What types of people or sizes of groups would you want to invite into this space? Dream big, and allow your sketches to be prayerful and playful. Create a space you'd like to create in!

The Adventure Begins

On June 1, 2021, we welcomed Ena as our first artist in residence, nervously helping her settle into a bedroom that didn't even have working electricity. Leaving our sweet girl in the house overnight was harder than I thought it would be. What if the water stopped working? What if she was too scared to fall asleep in that creaky building all alone? What if her fears were legitimate and there really *was* someone living in the basement, who had somehow slipped under our radar?

To our delight, Ena made it through the night . . . and many more nights after that. Not too long after, we moved in a whole cohort of other artists from across the country: a dancer named Clare, a photographer named Sean, a musician named Jude, and of course, Fernando and me. We spent those first few months growing in our crafts, friendship, and faith . . . while just trying to survive the hot summer nights without air conditioning.

I like to think that the things that gave our funny little home character helped us grow in character as well—especially the stovetop with only one knob. By God's grace, we made it through that entire summer with great memories (and without carbon monoxide poisoning). Around that same time, we advanced to the finals of Our Sunday Visitor's Innovation Challenge, providing us with much-needed funding. By fall, we were ready to welcome our second cohort to a house that felt a little bit more like a home and a program that felt a lot more like a community.

Covenantal Love

> By wisdom a house is built,
> And by understanding it is established;
> by knowledge the rooms are filled
> With all precious and pleasant riches.
>
> —Proverbs 24:3–4

Part of what distinguished our home from becoming just an arbitrary bunch of artistic roommates was the creation of our covenant. It wasn't written all at once but rather built by the little lessons we learned along the way about how to best support artists and how to best love our brothers and sisters in Christ. If time was our pen, experience was our ink, and we combined the two to write a set of guidelines that I think are worth sharing.

THE COVENANT OF ST. JOSEPH'S HOME FOR ARTISANS

We, the artists and missionaries of St. Joseph's Home for Artisans, prayerfully and unanimously vow to uphold the following charisms in our art, home, and community:

- » radical joy in the face of adversity;
- » unyielding grace in conflict, especially with fellow artists and the church community;
- » creativity without fear; and
- » humble obedience to the teachings of Jesus Christ and the social teachings of the Catholic Church.

We understand that we represent the St. Joseph's Home for Artisans and St. Leonard's as individuals and as a collective, and thus we agree to live our creative and personal lives in a way that honors our church and our home.

We seek to use our time in residency to better ourselves and our art for the sake of our world and our church. Knowing this, we pledge to create and communicate in a way that mirrors and honors our Creator.

In pursuit of purity of heart, we joyfully choose to remain close to the sacraments. Acknowledging the peace and unity that the sacraments bring to us as individuals and a community, we will encourage each other to use these gifts, especially Reconciliation and Holy Communion.

Fortified by friendship, we agree to create with humility, gratitude, and childlike wonder. Adopting the role of humble craftsman under an almighty Creator, we will pursue the true and good through beauty.

> St. Joseph:
> Mirror of justice,
> Lover of poverty,
> Model of artisans,
> Glory of home life—
> Pray for us.

Artist MOMENTS

Consider your creative community or the creative community you aspire to create (or join). What would the covenant of that community be like? What are the things you think will make this community flourish? What are the things you want to avoid? Use this space to write it out.

_____

_____

_____

_____

_____

_____

_____

_____

_____

_____

_____

_____

Interview with an Artist:
A TRIP DOWN MEMORY LANE
with Ena Dancy Urbalejo

For the first artist interview in this book, I knew I had to speak with that same brave girl who survived the first night in the residency alone. Ena Dancy Urbalejo is a musician, visual artist, and one of my best friends. Getting to build this artists' home was a gift, but getting to create it alongside Ena was pure privilege.

Sitting on that same couch we found on the street years ago, I asked Ena how creating this home affected her creative journey as a whole.

> I stopped feeling alone. I saw people who wanted to do something different with their lives and leave an impact in this world. And that influenced me to work

harder and make the sacrifices that others were doing to reach my full potential.

We chatted a bit about how much we had wanted acceptance and affirmation, and what it was like to "blend in" with the neighborhood where we had built our home. That meant getting in with the tight-knit, old-school Italians who had been living here forever. I felt that some people were quick to welcome us and others were more hesitant. Ena agreed.

> I felt I had to find my place in the neighborhood and community we were joining. We knew we were going to be affecting them, and that was scary and intimidating. It was a new place, and people had expectations of us. And I guess we had to be open to change. I feel we evolved from just creating what we thought people might like to actually doing the work of making connections, and through that more opportunities came of doing different things.

Reflection QUESTIONS

While not every artist has the opportunity to join the kind of intentional community described in this chapter, finding support and encouragement—particularly from other artists—can help us make the most of our creative gifts. Ask yourself the following:

- » What people has God put in your path to encourage you to use your creative gifts? Do you have the community and support you need?
- » What challenges ("black mold" stories) have you faced in creating and sustaining relationships with other artists?
- » Have you had any "rooftop" experiences, where you were overwhelmed by the possibilities?

1. Forming an intentional Covenant Community

Chapter 2

WHAT MAKES AN ARTIST?

> If you hear a voice within you say, "You cannot paint," then by all means paint, and that voice will be silenced.
>
> —Vincent Van Gogh

Years before I opened the artists' home, I moved to New York City to pursue poetry. On the occasional weekend when I could afford a break from the dog walking and nannying that paid my rent, I'd take the train out of the city and into the sweet little Jersey town of Warren. I was twenty-three, trying to rise to the challenge of "If you can make it there, you can make it anywhere" and failing miserably. And so, the New Jersey Transit became my reprieve, whisking me away on weekends from all the failed auditions and rejection letters and into the warm embrace of suburbia.

The best part of these weekends, besides having a break from the rats and ramen noodles, was getting to visit with my friend Katie's family. The Clementes are one of those families they make Christmas movies about: four generations under one roof. Things can get a little crazy, but at the end of every day, they still meet around the dinner table and hold hands when they say grace.

The real shining star of the family though was Katie's grandmother, or as I was honored to call her, "Grammy." She loved to talk, especially about her two favorite subjects: how much she loves her grandchildren and how much she loves beating her grandchildren at gin rummy. And so, I was a little startled when the conversation shifted, and she turned her full attention on me.

"So Clare," she would begin. "Tell me: what are you up to these days?"

I answered her almost unthinkingly—and with total honesty. "Well, Grammy, I quit my job. And I'm hoping to be . . ." I paused at the same spot I always pause at. "I want to be a writer."

I had expected a polite nod, but instead Grammy looked up from shuffling her cards, surprised. "I thought you *were* a writer?"

I blinked. "Well, Grammy," I sputtered, unprepared for a real conversation on how my dreams were going (or rather, weren't going). "Right now, I'm not a writer. I'm a camp counselor in Red Hook, and I babysit and dog walk on the side. I like to write, but it's not like I'm a real writer or anything."

Grammy's usual soft smile hardened for a moment, the billowy softness around her eyes becoming something more solid. "Well, then," she challenged me. "What *will* make you a real writer?"

Finally, an answer that came easily. "Once I'm supporting myself financially with writing. No day job, no babysitting gigs. I'll be a writer once I pay my bills with writing, and writing alone."

Her brows clicked together like knitting needles, pulling me apart at my seams and stitching me back together again. "So, being a writer has to do with making money?"

I tugged at the loose string of flawed logic she was dangling in front of me. "I guess it doesn't make sense that who I am would have anything to do with money."

Her questions raised the hem of my insecurities, exposing the shaking ankles barely holding up my self-image. Had I been defining "writer" all wrong? Had I been defining *myself* all wrong?

This conversation has stayed with me, and I've become happy to acquiesce to her idea that money has nothing to do with creativity, since apparently money wants nothing to do with me and my art either.

But then the question always circles back, mocking me to the beat of a ticking clock: *If making money from your artistry doesn't make you an artist, then what does?* How would *you* answer that question? Let's take a closer look at what Catholics believe about the purpose of art and beauty.

Artistry and the Transcendentals

Artists devote themselves to the transcendentals of beauty, truth, and goodness in a unique way, especially Christian artists, who aspire to create in the image of the Creator.

Artists live in service of *beauty*, instead of asking beauty to serve their own ambitions or satiate their desires. In this way, they make a gift of themselves. The true artist focuses more on producing than on consuming, which is part of what I got wrong in my early career. The pressures of the world dragged me into a headspace in which I prioritized what I could get from my gifts (money and recognition) over what I could give to my gifts and through my gifts.

Similarly, artists in general—and Catholic artists in a unique way—are devoted to eternal *truths*. The modern world encourages ego in creatives, telling us that our work must provide new answers to old questions, push boundaries, and disregard absolute truths in favor of "finding their own truth." To this end, the avant-garde and grotesque are often rewarded. But true artists understand that there are objective truths that transcend subjective opinions. This empowers them to enjoy the creative process even more than any delusions of a more malleable reality because they can play and create in the mysteries that enshroud and uplift those *eternal* truths. In the acceptance of the coexistence of truth and mystery comes creative freedom.

The transcendental that I've always struggled with the most, as a Catholic and as an artist, is *goodness*—something that is good to the degree that it fulfills its purpose. And so, the creative and consumer alike must ask, What is the purpose of art? In a world that reduces art to its monetary value, the definition of "good" begins to lose all meaning. The cynic (or the girl at her friend's grandma's kitchen table) could argue that art accomplishes its goal if it generates a profit. And if it accomplishes its goal, then it is good.

But now on the other side of that powerful conversation with Grammy all those years ago, I would argue that if an artist creates work that points the receiver toward the ultimate Artist and his work, then the artist has created something good.

Who can create something that meets all of these criteria? Is it only the most talented? Is it only the most prolific? Is it only the most celebrated?

No.

If the transcendentals serve as our measure of a "real" artist, a child can be just as "real" of an artist as a man or woman with a sixty-year career. And why shouldn't they be? In fact, I would argue that the greatest artists are those who never lose the wonder and humility that come with being a beginner.

Artist MOMENTS

Consider your most recent creative work. Does it meet the criteria of the transcendentals? You can use this rubric to deconstruct your work and figure it out.

IS THIS PIECE BEAUTIFUL?	
IS THIS PIECE TRUE?	
IS THIS PIECE GOOD?	

Always Be a Beginner

When I opened St. Joseph's Home for Artisans, as my friends and talented artists in residence started joining us from around the country, a disturbing pattern began to emerge. With a sense of irony that was not lost on me, I found that my fledgling artists refused to refer to themselves as *artists*. Some of the most enormously talented young people I've ever met told me that they would never call themselves *real* artists because creative work is just something they like to do for fun, as if fun is the gravestone that marks the death of professionalism.

Time and time again, I'd sit the artists down and plead with them to explain why they were refusing to call themselves what they so obviously were. And time and time again, I'd have my own prideful, self-indulgent excuses handed right back to me.

> "Well, I don't actually paint that often."
> "Well, I write, but I've never been published."
> "Well, I only sing at church."

Their self-deprecating comments brought me back to a particularly damning passage in G. K. Chesterton's *Orthodoxy*:

> What we suffer from today is humility in the wrong place. Modesty has moved from the organ of ambition. Modesty has settled upon the organ of conviction; where it was never meant to be. A man was meant to be doubtful about himself, but undoubting about the truth; this has been exactly reversed. The old humility was a spur that prevented a man from stopping: not a nail in his boot that prevented him from going on.

For the old humility made a man doubtful about his efforts, which might make him work harder. But the new humility makes a man doubtful about his aims, which will make him stop working altogether.[1]

Think about it. A person with a garden doesn't become a gardener when they grow their first prize-winning tomato. They become a gardener somewhere between the moment when they first suggest there might be something more worthy of planting in the backyard than cigarette butts and the moment two months later when they whisper words of encouragement to what everyone else swears is a blade of grass but they know for a fact is the beginnings of a beanstalk.

Similarly, an individual doesn't become an artist the first time they pay their electric bill by selling a painting. Getting your work published, as exciting as that may be, has very little to do with actually becoming a writer. It is instead the moment that your pen hits the paper—spilling out the words you know to be true, tracing the silhouette of stories you know to be beautiful, and fighting for the values you know to be good—that you become a writer.

Artist MOMENTS

Use this space to give yourself permission to think of yourself as an artist. Many artists write "Artist Statements" that explain who they are as creatives and what their practice centers on. Craft an artist statement that introduces you and your gifts by name.

Make Your Life a Masterpiece

What I'm trying to express to you can be expressed much more beautifully and clearly by a great saint, Pope John Paul II, who in his 1999 "Letter to Artists" is clear about where an individual's identity as an artist comes from. And this may shock you to read, but it has nothing to do with money or rate of creative output at all.

> Not all are called to be artists . . . yet all men and women are entrusted with the task of crafting their own life . . . to make of it a work of art, a masterpiece. The opening page of the Bible presents God as a kind of exemplar of everyone who produces a work: the human craftsman mirrors the image of God as Creator. . . . The one who creates bestows being itself, he brings something out of nothing—*ex nihilo sui et subiecti*, as the Latin puts it—and this, in the strict sense, is a mode of operation which belongs to the Almighty alone. The craftsman, by contrast, uses something that already exists, to which he gives form and meaning. This is the mode of operation peculiar to man as made in the image of God.[2]

God is the only true Creator because he made everything out of absolutely nothing. He describes the children God created in his image as "craftsmen." We are not just *able* but also *called* to shape what God already created into something beautiful, true, and good. And in our toil over these transcendentals, the hope is that we may be able to get a little bit closer to a view of the heaven that awaits, another masterpiece of our Creator's. In that act of crafting—or creating—we enrich not just our own lives but also the lives of all those we encounter by providing signs of hope in a world that is suffering on every level.

> As individuals, we are suffering from a lack of beauty.
> As a society, we are suffering from a lack of beauty.
> As a Church, we are suffering from a lack of beauty.
> And so, the question becomes, How do we fix it?

Well, I think Pope John Paul II was on to something. We are called to make our entire lives creative masterpieces; starting at the very ground level of the home, even in the simplest and most ordinary ways, we are called to use our talents, in the words of Thérèse of Lisieux, by "doing small things with great love."

Artist MOMENTS

For me, the first step toward a more beautiful world might be to sing while doing the dishes! What does this look like for you?

_____

_____

_____

_____

_____

_____

_____

_____

_____

Fearless First Steps

Perhaps the most revolutionary stand you could take against a culture of utilitarianism is to share your poetry with some friends in your home. Share your poetry *because* it won't bring you any closer to becoming rich and famous.

Or what if you auditioned for community theater? Would it be too embarrassing to admit that you wish you could be in a play again? Or could it be the one thing that reminds you that you were a child, created to play?

Would you ever consider drawing a self-portrait, all alone in your room? What type of person would you be if you began to carry around a small pack of watercolors every time you walked through the park? How would the most creative, childlike version of you live?

Not everyone is called to create for a living, but everyone is called to live in a way that is creative. And to me, that's the only metric that means anything. I sat down with my dear friend Trenée to learn how she honors Christ as the origin of her creativity.

Interview with an Artist:
TALKING ABOUT TRUTH
with Trenée McGee

The integration of Christianity and creativity is personified in my friend, Connecticut House of Representatives member Trenée McGee. Trenée is one of the youngest state representatives in the country and the owner of TDM Production and Acting Studio. She also just happens to be, as a Black female Democrat, one of the most passionate pro-life advocates in our country. Trenée is one of the most eloquent people I know, and the way she devotes her gifts to kingdom building humbles and inspires me.

I asked her what she believes makes an artist, and she told me that an artist is someone who can overcome obstacles by finding a creative way of telling that story, adding that a true artist is someone who "strives to be honest and a truth teller."

Trenée knows a thing or two about telling the truth in both creative and political spheres, even when it isn't popular. My dear friend exemplifies what it means to serve beauty, truth, and goodness before partisanships or special interests—even her own. This past year she introduced a theater tax credit bill, which incentivizes producers to bring their shows to Connecticut with a 30 percent tax write-off. Despite the extreme polarization rampant in politics, the majority voted yes and the bill passed, guaranteeing residents access to beauty right there in their home state.

To get both sides to unify almost unanimously is a rare feat, even rarer when the bill's champion is a relative newcomer to the political scene. She explained, "At the center of my artistry is God. I realized a long time ago that if I didn't put him at the center, I'd lose my foundation. People strive to be famous, but in reality, gaining the world and losing your soul is ultimately just death."

Trenée dedicates all of her creativity to God, and part of that means being open to the Holy Spirit at any and every moment. For her, inspiration often comes in the middle of a church service. "I'll have an idea and just have to grab an offering envelope and write it down."

Imagine that. An *offering envelope*, of all things.

Reflection QUESTIONS

» When do you think of yourself as a *real* artist?
» Where in your life do you find beauty?
» Where in your life do you find truth?
» Where in your life do you find goodness?
» Break out your own "offering envelope": what could you create if you stopped worrying about what other people might say?

Chapter 3

HOW TO MAKE IT LOOK AS IF YOU'RE HAVING FUN DANCING

(How I Broke out of Rigidity and Became a Creative . . . and How You Can Too)

> To dance is to be out of yourself. Larger, more beautiful, more powerful. This is power, it is glory on earth and it is yours for the taking.
> —Agnes de Mille

I don't know why I'm a bad dancer.

Growing up, I guess I had an inkling that dancing wasn't really my thing. Of course, coming of age in a farm town in Massachusetts, I wasn't really bothered by this; dancing wasn't really anyone else's thing either.

My first time at a school dance was in the basement of my parish church, St. James. I remember being *so excited* to be there, despite not really knowing a lot of the songs that caused the other kids to start screaming after just the first few lines. By eleven years old, I had already decided that the point of dances wasn't to jump around with your friends, wasn't to try on teenagerhood for a night, and wasn't even to show everyone how my gangly little body looked in something other than a school uniform. The point of going to dances was one thing and one thing only: slow dancing.

Slow dancing—there's something I could do. The rules were clear (as per my parents, with whom I had practiced at home before the dance): my hands go on his shoulders, and his go on the small of my waist, no higher and *definitely* no lower. Sway left, sway right. Let the lyrics of Savage Garden's "I Knew I Loved You" lead you around the linoleum floor under the watchful eye of a Pope John Paul II poster. Go ahead and get carried away in the moment, but not so much that you bump into the support beams planted randomly throughout the church basement. And do it all while your parents watch from the chaperone station at the door.

This I could do. As stilted as they were, the instructions were clear. And while slow dancing in a well-lit basement may have been a little uncomfortable, it didn't make me feel half as awkward as dancing to fast songs.

During the fast songs—from "Sk8r Boi" to "Pon de Replay"—it seemed everyone else knew how to throw their body around to the beat, not just going side to side but up and down and forward and back too. Their arms would fly up at what felt like the most unexpected times to me, but must have somehow been obvious to everyone else because they all seemed to do it in time with each other.

I scraped through middle school on slow dances and slow dances alone. Then high school came, and my old problem was swallowed whole by a bigger one. The good news was kids weren't making up crazy dance moves I couldn't keep up with anymore. The bad news was they had all switched over to grinding. And so, as you can imagine, four years passed without me ever really dancing at all. At homecoming, I volunteered to sell water bottles outside the gym. At prom, I mostly just sat and drank punch.

In college, I discovered that dances weren't so unbearable if I was drinking. The alcohol blurred out the edges of my rigidity. As someone whose greatest strength (and greatest weakness) is self-awareness, drinking allowed me to forget myself for a blessed hour or so. However, every moment of blissful self-forgetting was paid for in the morning with excruciating hours of painful self-remembering. From the way I became aware of every ounce of food inside my stomach to the way the light glaring through my lids offended my eyes, it became clear that this shortcut to ego abandonment wasn't worth it.

And that's the story of how I prolonged a problem—my inability to actually let go and enjoy dancing—for fifteen years. As an adult, I'd still go dancing if my friends insisted, but I refused to even try to enjoy it, which was too bad because it really did seem as if everyone else was having the time of their lives.

Well, *our* lives.

If it seemed as if I were smiling right alongside them, it was only a cruel symptom of that same self-awareness that propels and hinders me with equal force: I was painfully aware that if I didn't pretend to enjoy it, it would only draw attention to just how bad at dancing I am.

I was forced to confront this insecurity when I moved into the artists' home. Those darned artists . . . they were obsessed with dancing, and good at it too. Of course, it didn't help that my new best friends and roommates were all from places where even the trees and waves sway in time with the beat: Mexico, Puerto Rico, Dominican Republic, the Philippines . . . and of course, New Jersey! I'd beg off invitations to go to salsa and bachata clubs, but it didn't matter. The rhythm seemed to infiltrate our home—chores had a way of turning into dish-cleaning discos and shuffles to morning Mass into line dances. And much to my chagrin, for the first time in my life, I was surrounded by people who could not only dance but also spot a fake smile a mile away. When my smiles were fake, they knew before I even did.

So, I had to learn to like dancing. And by that, I mean I had to learn to like self-abandonment. With time, I was able to see my struggle to let go while dancing as an allegory for my struggle to let go in all different aspects of my life. As I learned how to take myself a little bit less seriously on the dance floor, I was able to apply those same lessons to my creative life as well.

Dancing Queen

As I mentioned, it took me fifteen years to begin confronting my fear of looking stupid while I danced. Once I did begin trying to enjoy myself, there was a lot of very public trial and error. And I suppose it wasn't making mistakes that I was so afraid of but rather the "in public" bit that had scared me off for so long.

If you had asked me what the worst thing was that could happen if I actually let go and had fun on the dance floor, I would have told you the absolute *worst* thing would be someone calling out how awkward I was in front of my friends or a boy I liked.

As it turns out, this fear applied to my art-making as well.

I began to write long before I began to feel comfortable sharing my work publicly—especially into a microphone. Call it insecurity, call it imposter syndrome, or call it spiritual attack—I was terrified that one day someone would point out what I had secretly suspected all along: I'm not particularly talented or even hardworking. And without those two key virtues, I didn't have a prayer of becoming a "real" writer.

I wish I could say those fears went away with time, with years of performance experience and publishing credits, but in reality, the only thing that actually helped assuage my worst fears was experiencing them coming true. Just as I suspected, there were people out there who were just dying to tell me how bad of a writer I am and how I should just give up and "get a real job."

Similarly, as I started letting go and jumping around on the dance floor with my friends, I encountered some sour personalities who delighted in pointing out how dumb I looked and even mimicking my awkward movements.

And both of these experiences, however momentarily painful, became blessings: they helped me not only filter whom I spend my time with but also realize that criticism really doesn't hurt as bad as I thought it would. Once I came to terms with the fact that not everyone was going to have (or needed to have) a positive perception of me, I found every form of self-expression to be easier and more joyful.

I Wanna Dance with Somebody

As veteran kindergarten teachers and wizened police chiefs can tell you, hurt people hurt people. To whatever degree others mock the way you dance or write or sing, you can assume they are ten times more critical of their own self-expression, frozen by the fear of failure and often censoring themselves into oblivion. Resentful of their own lack of courage to pursue their passions and talents, they project their insecurities onto those who do have the courage to fail boldly by constantly talking down about their own lack of skill (or exaggerating yours) to make sure that everyone around them feels just as small as they do.

The good news, though, is that confidence is just as contagious as insecurity.

One of the greatest catalysts for my learning to love dancing was finding the right dance partners. It's much easier to find ego abandonment when you're jumping up and down next to someone who doesn't take themself too seriously. Similarly, as a creative, I've found that those who believe in themselves and their own work want nothing more than for me to believe in my vocation. It is, in the truest sense of the word, the kind of relationship that C. S. Lewis wrote about in his classic work *The Four Loves*.

Friendship, writes Lewis, is a kind of companionship in which "one or more of the companions discover that they have in common some insight or interest or even taste which the others do not share and which, till that moment, each believed to be his own unique treasure (or burden)." For the artist, this translates into chasing beauty, truth, and goodness through the particular medium of their choice—and yet they undeniably share the pursuit in common, just like the hunter (or in his case, the scholar). Lewis continues: "The typical expression of opening Friendship would be something like, 'What? You too? I thought I was the only one.' . . . It is when two such persons discover one another, when, whether with immense difficulties and semi-articulate fumblings or with what would seem to us amazing and elliptical speed, they share their vision—it is then that Friendship is born."[1]

My best friendships are with my fellow creatives who don't laugh at me when something I create fails. They also don't lie to me and pretend everything I write is worthy of publishing. More than just "believing in me," they believe in the purpose and gifts that God has given me—yet they also recognize my fallibility as an artist and an individual, and don't just blindly support me in everything I do. These friendships are rare but necessary for any creative person because they are based on *truth*.

So, how do you go about finding friends like this? In the art world and beyond, it can be so hard to find trusted friends who will abandon both snark and flattery, and just give you the plain old truth. My suggestion? Look for people who always tell *themselves* the truth. Those who are in love with the truth will insist upon it for themselves, even when it's uncomfortable, and when they love you, they'll insist on it for you too.

For what it's worth though, this is the one part of my metaphor that doesn't extend to my dancing as well. If I look like a baboon trying to reach an itch during the Cupid Shuffle, don't tell me.

Artist MOMENTS

What makes the ideal friend, co-creator, and dance partner for you? Use this space to map out those qualities, and jot down some of the names of friends, family, and collaborators who are fulfilling that need. Consider using this space to write them a note of gratitude.

_____

_____

_____

_____

_____

_____

_____

_____

_____

_____

Am I on the Right Track?

As we continue to fight this internal battle over whether we feel confident in ourselves or in our art, or find friends, companions, and allies who have embarked on a similar quest, we must never lose sight of the fact that our ultimate sense of purpose is rooted not in ourselves but in God alone.

How can we know we are on the right track? The answer, as always, can be found in scripture. "Finally, beloved, whatever is true, whatever is honorable, whatever is just, whatever is pure, whatever is pleasing, whatever is commendable, if there is any excellence and if there is anything worthy of praise, think about these things. Keep on doing the things that you have learned and received and heard and seen in me, and the God of peace will be with you" (Phil 4:8–9).

A self-referential confidence that transcends no higher than your own abilities and no deeper than your own reflection will always be not only shallow but also unsustainable. As a creative, putting your faith in your ability to create work—especially work that receives external validation—is a dangerous, losing game. The only safe place to place your confidence is in the Word himself.

As Philippians 4:8 reminds us, place your confidence in whatever is true, honorable, pure, pleasing, commendable, excellent, and worthy of praise. When we use these tools, we honor the legacy the Creator has crafted for us and, abandoning our confidence to something greater than ourselves, are empowered to make our most beautiful work.

Artist MOMENTS

Use the chart below to examine your own practice according to the rubric given to us by Philippians 4:8. Try to go beyond a simple yes or no answer and examine why your work does or does not meet these criteria.

IS MY WORK TRUE?	
IS MY WORK HONORABLE?	
IS MY WORK JUST?	
IS MY WORK PURE?	
IS MY WORK PLEASING?	
IS MY WORK COMMENDABLE?	
IS MY WORK EXCELLENT?	
IS MY WORK WORTHY OF PRAISE?	

Good Vibrations

While we can easily list the beautiful qualities described in Philippians 4:8, truly understanding what they mean in the context of our art-making can be tricky.

When we speak about the transcendentals, we often rush over "goodness" because it can feel a little harder to define than "beauty" and "truth." But for those of us who have ever struggled with insecurity about our creative gifts, the key to confidence may be in gaining a better understanding of what *goodness* really is.

For something to be *good*, it simply has to accomplish its purpose. Knowing this helps us reframe the question "Is what I'm creating good?" into something more manageable: "Does what I'm creating accomplish its purpose?"

Artist MOMENTS

What is the purpose of your personal creative work? Do you feel it's being accomplished? Use this space for your musings on goodness.

_____

_____

_____

_____

If we as people of faith agree that the only real purpose of anything is to glorify God, then anything we create that builds his kingdom on earth is worthy of creation. The world tries to grant artists freedom and confidence by insisting that all art is subjective, but I disagree. Ultimate creative freedom is achieved through not nihilistic subjectivity but the joyful acceptance that our work's goodness is determined by an objective reality that is (blessedly) so much bigger than ourselves.

Of course, there is value in doing something well. If my writing is excellent—not only creatively but also grammatically—it's going to reach more people. But even the roughest sketch or simplest phrase has the power to move hearts toward Christ if it is done with the pure intention of glorifying God.

This is easier said than done. These days, while I'm a confident writer, I'm still a bit of a bashful dancer. To learn a little bit more about how to be a *good* dancer, I spoke with

How to Make It Look as if You're Having Fun Dancing

my friend Autumn Phillips, a professional choreographer and dance instructor.

Interview with an Artist:
DANCING THE NIGHT AWAY
with Autumn Phillips

Curious about how other artists overcome self-consciousness not just in their dancing but also in all their art-making, I talked with my friend Autumn.

"At our core, we are all naturally inclined to be wary of vulnerability," she told me. "And dancing, especially in front of others, is an extremely vulnerable activity. However, while dancing, I always make sure to remind myself why I am doing this. There is almost always a deeper purpose to artistic movement, and holding fast to that purpose helps the fear to dissipate."

I wanted to know more about why Autumn dances. If something is *good* when it accomplishes its purpose, what is the purpose of dancing?

> Ultimately I am dancing for the purpose of storytelling. The story aches to be told, and my dance is necessary to make that happen. When my dancing becomes part of something greater than myself, I am able to take a step back and ignore the voice in the back of my mind telling me to be afraid. Afraid of what? Other people? Their thoughts? More often than not, I'm my own worst critic.
>
> So it doesn't matter what other people may think. No one else will be as critical as I am. At the end of the day, it's more important that I share the story with its audience and hope that they will be touched through this story. Even outside of the performance and storytelling aspect, I remind myself that I am blessed to be able to dance. Dance is a gift, and I need to embrace it and celebrate it, rather than hold myself back out of self-conscious fear. Simply put, I allow myself to melt into the movement and focus on the greater purpose and gift that dancing truly is.

I like Autumn's definition of dancing as storytelling, and I wonder if I might get a little bit more confident on the dance floor if I remember whose story I'm telling. Maybe when I make it less about me, I'll find more confidence in movement—and maybe I'll be able to apply that to other creative outlets too.

Reflection QUESTIONS

- » Do I create more for the process or for the product? Do I need to refocus or adjust that creative balance to achieve the real purpose of my art?
- » Have I ever experienced a negative reaction or review? How did it help me improve my craft?
- » How does the virtue of humility affect my pursuit of the beautiful, true, and good? Is it a spur or a nail in my boot?
- » How does Philippians 4:8 apply to my work? Is it true, honorable, just, pure, pleasing, commendable, excellent, and worthy of praise?
- » When I create, whose stories am I telling?

Chapter 4

FEED THE HUNGER INSIDE YOU

(The Gift of Hunger—Both Physical and Psychic—in the Life of a Creative)

> Heaven and earth, the Celtic saying goes, are only three feet apart, but in thin places that distance is even shorter. They are places that make us feel something larger than ourselves, as though we are held in a place between worlds, beyond experience.
>
> —Kerri ní Dochartaigh

Have you ever experienced an internal quiet that somehow, impossibly, roared in your ears? Have you ever felt a breeze ripple through the loose strand falling down from your ponytail and recognized it as more spirit than mere wind? Have you ever gone too long without letting the ocean touch your skin, only to find the laps of waves against your ankles feel more like fire than water?

Have you ever allowed yourself to believe, if only for a moment, that you accidentally touched the eternal?

There's a Christian Celtic term for this experience and the spaces that facilitate them: "thin places." These are the places and moments when the walls between heaven and earth grow so thin they're practically permeable, giving the individual access to the divine that is beautiful, brutal, and brief. Eric Weiner, author of the acclaimed book *Man Seeks God*, describes thin spaces as "places that beguile and inspire, sedate and stir, places where, for a few blissful moments I loosen my death grip on life, and can breathe again. . . . They are locales where the distance between heaven and earth collapses and we're able to catch glimpses of the divine, or the transcendent or, as I like to think of it, the Infinite Whatever."[2]

This Celtic understanding of thin places has been refuted by Christian thinkers many times over, and rightfully so. God is equally present to us everywhere. But are we—especially those of us trying to create in union with him—equally present to *him* everywhere *we* go?

And that's where the Celtic understanding falls short, I think. A true thin space isn't a physical place at all but rather a disposition. While he is ready to receive us always and anywhere, thin spaces are places where *we're* able to be open to *him* in an exceptional way.

The cloistered nun knows this, and the bedridden child knows this. The stay-at-home mom knows this, and the soldier deployed to the last place anyone would want to be knows this.

Travel is a beautiful opportunity to learn and grow, but intimate encounters with the divine aren't exclusive to those with big budgets and no fear of flying. In fact, I'd argue that the more in love with the world you are, the more likely you are to be captured within its walls. When you see the enclosure of "worldliness" as comfort instead of constraint, you're less likely to press against its walls and find the weak spots.

Christians can be empowered by this because we know that Christ and his kingdom thirst for us. So when we sense a great space between heaven and earth, we can rest assured that it's the fallen nature of earth that is pulling us from the yearning arms of heaven and not the other way around. If we want to adopt the disposition of closeness to not only Christ but also beauty, then that's up to us.

So, how does all of this empower the artist?

Well, God, as the Creator, is the author of all beauty. And so, any intimate encounter we can have between his home and ours enables us to write and paint a little bit more like him and bring a little bit more of that divine down here to earth.

Artist **MOMENTS**

Use this space to map out the separation between the world you've created for yourself and heaven. Where do you feel there is a thinness between the two? Is it a physical place, a relationship, or a set of habits? Describe it on the lines provided.

1. Created in union with God.

_____

_____

_____

_____

_____

Getting to the Thin Place (without Leaving Your Neighborhood)

A word of caution: If you're lucky enough to enter into this thin space, it feels a little like looking God in the eyes, which is to say, the pain is exquisite, addicting, and exhausting.

Allowing yourself to abandon the protective numbness that overstimulation usually provides can be a shock to the system. When you're so used to experiencing life with a buffer between you and your senses, allowing for rawness can be painful. The moments in which I lean into the thin space have been a maddening marriage of ecstatic gratitude and, ironically, the desperate urge to escape for the simple reason that my goodness, beauty *hurts*.

Pope Benedict XVI (then Cardinal Ratzinger) was perhaps more familiar with the wounding power of beauty than anyone else. In an address to an assembly of Communion and Liberation members, he said, "Whoever believes in God . . . knows that beauty is truth and truth beauty; but in the suffering Christ he also learns that the beauty of truth also embraces offense, pain, and even the dark mystery of death, and that this can only be found in accepting suffering, not in ignoring it."[1]

Well-intentioned artists may, upon reading this, consider building themselves a home in the thin space and living in that sensitive space perpetually in pursuit of creative greatness or holiness or both. Perhaps there are those who have done this successfully, but none that I know of. In our fallen state, touching the clouds feels like touching a live wire: exhilarating, painful, and quite literally deadly—because in order to unify with heaven, we have to leave our earthly bodies behind. Someday we'll be able to live in perpetual intimacy with beauty, but not yet.

So, how do we find these "thin spaces" that will allow us to satiate our hunger for divine connection, to inspire us and feed our souls? Let's look at three practical ways we can rebuild our sensitivity and unite ourselves to beauty.

Fasting

I don't know a greater impediment to accessing the thin space than overstimulation. If you desire to be wounded by beauty, then you can consider overstimulation the most effective shield you'll ever wield.

Overstimulating yourself—through noise, food and alcohol, screen time, or socialization—guarantees you won't have to ever worry about feeling the piercing arrow of beauty. You'll be too numbed to even notice when the divine is pushing against the divide, reaching out and offering you inspiration.

But what if you're already at that point and need a way to "dial back"? One of the most effective tools in combating overstimulation and cultivating sensitivity is *fasting*. When we fast, we unite with Moses on the mountain and Jesus in the desert. Like them, as we deny ourselves physical comforts and distractions, we become more aware of God's voice. As artists, being in intimate, frequent communication with the great Commissioner of our work is invaluable.

There is a time and place for fasting, as long as we have a clear and healthy understanding of *why* we're doing it. While there is the option to just reduce the quantity that we eat and drink, there's also something to be said—as creatives and Christians—for limiting the richness of our appetites lest we desensitize our tastes to the point of not being able to taste anything at all.

Of course, the perversion of our appetites goes far beyond our bellies. Our appetites for television, music, and even socialization can all be either overindulged or overregulated to the point that we lose our sensitivities and thus our openness to inspiration, from our fellow humans or from the divine.

One of the clearest examples of this in our culture is our perpetual need to keep our headphones in and radios blasting. In our incessant avoidance of even a moment of quiet, we ensure that if inspiration tries to reach us, we won't even be able to hear it. Many people go even further with this strategy, overscheduling themselves to guarantee that they never have to spend a moment alone with themselves.

Artist MOMENTS

What are some things you could fast from, as an investment in your creative practice?

_____

_____

_____

_____

_____

_____

_____

_____

_____

_____

In order to adopt the disposition of the thin space, we have to do something that our fallen world cautions against: we must allow ourselves to feel the *ache*, the ache of silence, the ache of hunger, and the ache of loneliness.

These longings remind us that this world isn't enough for us because we aren't made for this world. And in that longing—that ache—is the same stinging wound that Pope Benedict XVI speaks of when he speaks of beauty.

Go into Creation

Another important way to enter into the thin space is to venture into nature.

If God is the sole Creator and we are craftspeople who can create only from what he's already made, then no art can be made without using him not only as inspiration but also as paint, brush, and palette. Imagine that—every ounce of ink that pours from your pen was created by God; every instrument you play, anointed by him. It's much easier to recognize his handiwork in the trees and the rivers because they come so much more directly from him, but he is in all things.

And so, a great place to start is by entering into nature, in silence. Allow the quiet contact with creation to mend any desensitization from overstimulation. Turn off your phone and allow yourself to be a child, playing in the Father's garden. So much of our creative processes and output have been sanitized and regimented, and while structure can be an important part of the artist's life, meditative time in nature is imperative for those trying to reflect the abundant wilderness of God in their art.

Artist MOMENTS

Where is a quiet, meditative environment in which you can find peace and inspiration?

_____

_____

_____

_____

_____

_____

_____

The Sacraments

Finally, the sacraments are the ultimate opportunity for closeness with the divine—the Eucharist especially. What an indescribable gift, holding the Creator within us as we create!

Confession is a gift to the artist as well. According to the *Catechism*, "Sin is before all else an offense against God, a rupture of communion with him" (*CCC* 1440). So, going to Confession heals the rupture and keeps us close to our Creator, the source of all inspiration.

If our soul is sick, our attempts at creating beauty—no matter how well intentioned—will be tainted by the weight of what our soul was carrying. Unburdening yourself of sin before creating is a gift not only to yourself but also to your audience.

Shame and sin desensitize our souls. Our reactions to beauty, truth, and goodness are tempered by our ties to our vices. Confession enables us to clear the noise and reclaim the peace we need to create again.

Artist MOMENTS

How could increasing participation in the sacraments aid your creativity?

_____

_____

_____

_____

_____

_____

_____

Why Bother?

If this quest for beauty in the "thin spaces" is such a painful process, you have to ask, why should we even bother? Pope Benedict XVI had some insight into this:

> Is there anyone who does not know Dostoyevsky's often quoted sentence: "The Beautiful will save us"? However, people usually forget that Dostoyevsky is referring here to the redeeming Beauty of Christ. We must learn to see Him. If we know Him, not only in words, but if we are struck by the arrow of his paradoxical beauty, then we will truly know him, and know him not only because we have heard others speak about him.[2]

Choosing sensitivity in an often cruel and terrifying world is brave. The temptation to toughen yourself is understandable. But the graces on the other end of allowing yourself to be pierced by beauty far outweigh the suffering it may cost you. I have one friend, more than any other, who embodies this courage. Her name is Queen.

Interview with an Artist:
ON CHILDLIKE JOY
with the Beautiful Queen Carberry Banda

Queen Carberry Banda is a TED Talk presenter, journalist, author, and television personality. But when I first met her, she was just a new friend at leadership camp. I found an old picture of us during that summer—all gangly limbs and metal smiles—and I showed it to her. She laughed and said, "Good news is, time has been extremely kind."

That was an incredible thing to say if you know her story.

Born and raised in Tanzania, Queen lost her mother and twin siblings at age five. She described the days that followed their funerals as the last time she was allowed to be innocent, before she was subjected to years of abuse by the extended family she would be sent to live with. In the few weeks after the funerals, before she was sent to live with her abusers, she was allowed to live at Morogoro Seminary, where she spent her days learning how to read a newspaper, exploring the land, and getting happily lost in the neighborhood. As she told me, "When the sun got too hot, I found comfort and a snack under a baobab tree. Clare, I was more than happy in [the] seminary; I was at peace, a type of peace that I haven't been able to find anywhere."

I told her a little bit about my musings on thin spaces and whether they're actually places or a disposition of the spirit. I asked her if that was what that childhood oasis meant to her.

> Even when I think of where I would like to die and take my last breath, it's that place. There, I was actually able to celebrate and be a child. I was able to be as naive and sweet and clueless as I could possibly be. I was so intentionally vulnerable, and nothing bad happened. I was able to take my last few innocent breaths before it was all taken away from me. When I think of that place, I think of the purest side of me. Each time I go there, I feel that. I feel me, without the taintedness.

Obviously, while I respect Queen's words, I do not see my friend as tainted. I think she has the purest spirit I've ever known. Whether she recognizes it in herself or not, she embodies childlike joy and wonder in a way everyone around her hopes might just rub off on them too.

We finished our conversation by wondering aloud if there's something to the fact that she feels the most like herself—as a woman and a creative—when she feels childlike. I've noticed a lot of my friends feel that way, and I know it's how I feel too. Maybe it's because when you strip artists of everything else, we are all just children trying to look like our dad.

Reflection QUESTIONS

» When you read Queen's story, is there a place you think of that has a similar sense of belonging and childlike happiness for you? Can you recall encountering that feeling of being extra close to the divine?
» What have you found to be the best way to tune into silence?
» Do you consider yourself a "sensitive" person? Does leaning into sensitivity make you feel uncomfortable?
» What tempers your creativity? How do you avoid that?
» Under what conditions do you create your best work?

Chapter 5

MAKING SPACE

> A time to seek, and a time to lose; a time to keep, and a time to throw away.
> —Ecclesiastes 3:6

About a year ago, our neighbors donated a beautiful antique hutch to the artists' home. The hutch stands at a statuesque six feet tall and four feet wide but balances on short, muscular, bowed legs with ease. Thin strips of mahogany curl across the glass of its face like tendrils, giving it the appearance of someone shy but lovely. Above its mop of spirals and kinks, the hutch's apex forms what, in the right light, really does look like a tiara.

It's understated yet ornate, a hundred years old but in almost perfect condition. In fact, it is absolutely perfect, except that it's way too big for our house. A priceless antique reduced to mere hallway obstruction, it has sat at the entrance of our home for an entire year.

In my defense, it was just too beautiful not to accept, especially as it was free and being given by such wonderful friends. Also in my defense, do you know how hard it is to say no to inanimate objects when you're the type of right-brainer who personifies living room furniture?

But all excuses aside, I suppose that deep down, I always knew that the hutch wouldn't fit in our small space. In fact, despite its objective goodness and beauty, the hutch was crowding us and taking up valuable space that we could be using in ways that aligned with our mission. Both literally and metaphorically, it was blocking our entrance and keeping good things—things that might actually fit a whole lot better—from being able to come inside.

Around the same time that I was trying to discern what to do with my lovely but impractical hutch, I was dealing with some sort of interior blockage. After years of praying for the strength and courage to rise above my old limitations—physically, socially, emotionally, and spiritually—God had begun to give me everything I ever asked for. Quickly though, it became clear that in order to accept these new blessings, I would need to release my grip on the old blessings. Those old gifts weren't bad, outdated, or unusable, but they were obstructing my entrance and blocking the new gifts from entering.

In short, God wasn't asking me to throw away the hutch, but he was telling me to get it out of the hallway or spend the rest of my life having to suck it in as I squeeze through our hallway, stubbing and splintering, for no cause greater than my own stubbornness and sentimentality.

Space and the Artist

Now what does all of this have to do with the artist? The artist needs even more space than the average person because they need space not just to exist within but also to *create*. A painter doesn't paint on an already-filled canvas, and a musician can't compose with TV blaring in the background. In the emptiness, the artist finds possibility.

What exactly is that emptiness? Well, it can be physical space, social space, emotional space, or even spiritual space.

But knowing where to stow a bulky piece of furniture is a little bit easier than knowing how to rearrange and declutter your life, internally and externally.

Creating Physical Space

The precious gift of physical space is colloquially referred to as "studio space" among artists. When I began writing and performing, I'd crawl out onto the fire escape outside my fifth-floor apartment and, floating a couple hundred feet above Brooklyn, practice my poems for an audience of pigeons. It wasn't glamorous (or even particularly safe), but it was a space—a private, empty air space where I could create without fear of judgment or ridicule. Not too much longer down the line, I was given some studio space at an art residency in the woods of Washington. The campus was made up of a collection of quaint little cabins and included a pottery studio, a weaving studio, and a printmaking studio—but they didn't know where to put a spoken word poet.

So, I was given domain over the empty stained-glass studio. Every day, I would shuffle through the mounds of snow and write in a long rectangular shed that was empty except for thousands and thousands of cuts of colored glass. As the bright fluorescent lighting bounced off the snowy windows and onto the greens, blues, and pinks around me, I felt nurtured by the beauty and tranquility. Spoiled with space, I was able to create more than I had ever created before. I was completely won over by the effect that physical space had on my art-making process and promised to someday find a way to provide that not only for myself but also for others. So in many ways, the creation of St. Joseph's

Home for Artisans all those years later wasn't so much of a surprise as a process fulfilled.

But giving the artists space to live in wasn't enough. After a while, it became clear that we were outgrowing our tight living quarters. Our living room, kitchen, and even bedrooms were overflowing with easels, acoustic guitars, and worn-out copies of *The Screwtape Letters*. We were bursting, and gloriously so! But we were also crowding each other out. As I tried to focus on writing while one artisan practiced opera arias and another teetered on the leg of our couch so they could paint a design on the ceiling, I knew the time had come. St. Joseph's Home for Artisans needed studio space, badly.

As I had years before, I once again returned to Fr. Michael and asked if there was any more space at the proverbial inn. To my delight, he told me that there was an empty tower attached to the church that was currently just being used as storage space. If we could clean out all of the debris and bric-a-brac that had accumulated, we could use the tower as studio space.

The process of physically cleaning out the space was as meditative as it was sweaty and exhausting. God seems to get a giggle out of giving us five-story walk-ups, so we spent a week carrying old, abandoned furniture, statues, and tools down flights of wobbly stairs and out to the curb. In the emptiness that followed, we were able to clean the piles of dust and rust to reveal gorgeous wood flooring. Once it was cleaned, we began to move in desks and shelving, even building a small library and photography studio.

The addition of this studio space changed our program entirely. Simple, sparse studios became the artists' blank canvases, and the work they were able to create once given the space to do so was tenfold what they had been able to make before. However, we never would have been able to provide them with that space if we hadn't gone through the hard work of releasing the old clutter and dust to make space for new creations.

Artist MOMENTS

What would your dream studio be like? Use this space to draw the floor plan. Don't be afraid to dream big!

Creating Social Space

This next section is one of the hardest ones for me to write because, if there's one thing I love, it's my people. I consider myself fiercely loyal and am a big believer in chosen family, especially as a Body of Christ. However, I wish I had understood the malleable nature of relationships sooner, especially as an artist.

To be a creative is to be in a constant state of growth and experimentation. Often, dreaming up your next book, painting, or song requires a singularity of vision that can be, well, isolating. Especially when it comes to your less creatively inclined friends, your vision can be received with laughter or even a well-intentioned but patronizing concern. They don't mean any harm; they just see the world very differently than you do. And sometimes their attempts to protect their artist friends can manifest as attempts to coax them out of creative risk-taking.

As you step into your role as a craftsman, it may make others in your life—especially those who aren't accustomed to seeing you in that way—uncomfortable. You may be surprised at the things it causes them to say and do, and you may leave the conversation lonelier than if you had just stayed home alone.

When I consider the value of creating social space for yourself, I think of Noah and his ark. When I began my spoken word career in New York, a lot of the people whom I thought would be excited for me were actually the first ones to try to dissuade me from my path. I can now look back on it with a gentle and understanding heart. They knew this path wouldn't be easy, and I believe they were trying to save me from the sacrifice and heartache it would take. However, what I needed wasn't a way out but rather a fellowship of friends and family who could believe in my vision even when they couldn't see it themselves. Ironically, I processed the isolating feeling through poetry, writing a spoken word piece about it:

> Clear blue skies as far as the clear blue eyes can see,
> Not a cloud, not a drop.
>
> And while the rest of the village thinks today's for a walk in the park,
> I'd say today's a damn good day to start on my ark.
>
> Everyone's saying that I'm crazy,
> that the clouds ain't even a maybe.
>
> The clouds are a no,
> the sunshine's a go.
>
> They say:
> "If there's never been a flood before,
> Why would God have a flood in store?"
> I don't even try to prove myself to them anymore.
>
> I don't need approval,
> I just need
> a hammer & a nail.
>
> This ark,
> is built to fail.
>
> Because its builder,
> was built to fail.
>
> But then to try again!

(after, crying again)
I'll rip it board by board,
go back to that hard times hardware store
—and I'll start again.

Until this ark is no longer built to fail!
Until this ark is built to sail.

Listen,
It doesn't really even have to be a boat,
It just sorta has to, kinda float.

Neighbor said, "You're bound to fail when you build
    an ark without a manual."
But what neighbor doesn't know is that my manual,
I've just been readin' my bible backwards,
a rewinded tape of God's great word,

'cause I've been the hammer and nail in the
    Passion—
but now I wanna be the hammer and nail in Genesis,
    so an ark I'll fashion—

I'll build it for you,
the God who tells me it's gonna rain
when everyone else tells me:
"Girl, you've gone insane!"

Build it for you!
The Lord of dreams that don't make sense,
because you are the Father of recompense.

You wouldn't have me toil,
if you weren't planning on watering this soil.

Making Space

So this is, what I'll do:
I'll build the ark.

And I'll be generous with its doors,
swing 'em open like my arms.

I don't want two of every animal,
I just need, to be joined by whoever will.

'Cause the goal isn't to end up on my ark alone,
The goal is to find fellow sailors tryna get
home.

Through art and that business you've secretly always
  dreamed of.
Through music,
and that talent you know you have, but never speak
  of.
And why would you?

Your Life is fine as is,
no need for,
Genesis.

But today, while I have your attention,
I'm gonna pass you a hammer and nails,
throw wrench in—

Friend!
Build your ark, on the sunniest day you can find.
Build the ark on Junes and Julys.

The greatest arks are built by the craziest people—
The greatest kingdoms by those even crazier still.

Build it in the light,
do not wait for the dark.

On the sunniest day you can find—
build
your
ark.

Though it terrified me, I had no choice but to build a new social circle for myself—one that not just understood my vision but could add to it. It also helped a lot that these new friends, often artists themselves, were creating their own visions alongside me, inspiring me to fight even harder for my own.

Of course, I didn't simply throw away the relationships (many of them lifelong). I just found ways to restructure my life and relationships so I wouldn't be putting such tremendous pressure on relationships that weren't built to hold the weight of my new art-making. I learned that not everyone can offer me everything, especially the kind of support I needed as a fledgling creative. Accepting this allowed me freedom for myself and grace for my loved ones.

Artist MOMENTS

Are there relationships that cause more harm than good to your creative work? Allow yourself the space below to examine those relationships with an honest and graceful heart.

_____

_____

_____

_____

_____

_____

_____

_____

_____

_____

_____

Emotional Space

Many artists are super-feelers. Their empathy is their superpower because it allows them to relate not only to their own pain but also to others'. From this, they can write piercing melodies and complex characters that would be otherwise impossible for them to construct. But this great strength is also their great weakness: if they aren't careful, their sensitivities to the emotional stresses and needs of those around them can overtake them.

For many artists, this can result in being overwhelmed by anxiety or exhausted by their own people-pleasing tendencies. I'm not saying that artists shouldn't give of themselves emotionally, especially to those they have personal relationships with. Rather, I'm suggesting that artists have to be especially intentional with their emotional expenditures since some of that heart space needs to be reserved for art-making. This may sound a little selfish, but when you understand art-making as a way to make a gift of yourself, it becomes clear that it's simply another way of budgeting your emotional expenditures so you don't run out in your relationships or your art-making.

Artist MOMENTS

Has anything in your life been draining you emotionally? How has that affected your art-making? Write about it here.

_____

_____

_____

_____

_____

_____

Creating Spiritual Space

Finally, artists need spiritual space in order to create. Of course, the first and best way to clear out that space in the soul is the Sacrament of Reconciliation. Not unlike the section on clearing out physical space, Confession removes the junk—often junk that we've let ourselves become pretty attached to—and makes space for the divine inspiration and movements of the spirit that allow our work to transcend ourselves. Sometimes, we become accustomed to our own spiritual blockages because we've carried them for so long. But if we just give them over to God with a contrite heart, we will not just please and be reunited with him but also have the opportunity to restore our relationship with the inspiration he wants to give us.

Clearing spiritual space can also look like letting go of disordered attachments we insist on holding onto, even to our own detriment. These can range from attachments to disordered relationships to the materialist attachment to *stuff, stuff, and more stuff*. Like reconciliation, this release of spiritual attachments can be understood through the metaphor of physical attachments. When we try to fill the ache within our hearts with cheap substitutes, we may be temporarily appeased, but we will never be satiated. For the artist especially, it would be better to just live alongside the ache, using it as a well to create from, rather than trying to temporarily pacify it.

Artist MOMENTS

What might be taking up too much space for you spiritually? How would you go about freeing that space for yourself? Using the space below, allow yourself to mix words and drawings to visualize the difference in what your spirit looks like with and without that blockage.

Discernment ✱

My suggestion, as you begin to discern what is and isn't serving your vocation as a creative, is to abandon yourself—and your desires—to the Lord and his plan. Whatever is right for you and your path as an artist, God will provide for.

There is a simple prayer that is often prayed among fed-up twentysomethings looking for love: "God, if they aren't the one, please remove them from my life." I think it applies to the artist trying to practice discernment as well: "God, if this isn't what you've intended for me, please remove it from my life."

Not that God needs our permission, but it sure does help when we surrender to his plan instead of fighting him every step along the way. When I consider the idea of submitting to God's plan and creating space, I think of the youngest artist in residence to ever come through our residency's doors: Adam Moniz.

Interview with an Artist:
MAKING A MURAL
with Adam Moniz

Adam Moniz is an oil painter and muralist from Fall River, Massachusetts. He went to school for illustration but soon realized that his gifts could be used in even broader ways.

When I first received Adam's application, I balked at the age written on the top right-hand corner. He was way below the age range I had set for the program, in an attempt to circumvent young artists' experimental years. But I hopped on a video call to humor him and, to my delighted surprise, was completely blown away by his old soul. Combined with his incredible portfolio, I had no choice but to break my own rules and make space for God's plan instead of mine.

Since then, his blank canvases have ranged from the two-story window-front of a bank to a pair of customized Converse shoes. Adam sees every blank space as an opportunity to make something beautiful, which is why I knew I had to speak with him about this chapter.

In particular though, I wanted to ask Adam about his work as a muralist because that medium deals with such massive amounts of blank space. "When I'm looking to paint a mural, I'm drawn to open space." He likened it to the doodles he used to draw in his college-lined notebooks. "I just focus on filling in the spaces. With doodling, I can use the infrastructure of the paper and just focus on filling in the space. And when I'm painting a mural, I just use the infrastructure of the building."

I can't imagine what it's like to see the world through Adam's eyes—where every blank wall or T-shirt is a canvas waiting to be filled. He described it as "taking everything in and then your art is just the act of letting everything out." His words conjured within me an image of creative work as the inhale of inspiration and the exhale of art.

How would my life look if I saw emptiness as canvas and blank space as opportunity to create? Could I train inspiration to move through me as freely and naturally as breath? Would abandoning my expectations, as I had to in order to bring my talented friend Adam into our program, be the only way to allow that breath of the Holy Spirit to move through me?

Reflection QUESTIONS

- » Which parts of your life do you need more space in? Do you need space socially, emotionally, spiritually, intellectually, or physically?
- » What are practical ways that you could create that space?
- » What's holding you back from removing your creative blockades?
- » If you were to imagine your creative work as a breath, what would you be inhaling and what would you be exhaling?
- » What would a mural of your life look like?

Chapter 6

SUCCESS IS THE BEST REVENGE

(Handling Both Success and Defeat as a Christian Creative)

> Optimism is a wish without warrant; Christian hope is a certainty, guaranteed by God himself. Optimism reflects ignorance as to whether good things will ever actually come. Christian hope expresses knowledge that every day of his life, and every moment beyond it, the believer can say with truth, on the basis of God's own commitment, that the best is yet to come.
>
> —J. I. Packer

While it's been explained to me that most people are not overnight successes, I secretly always assumed that I would be the exception. And there, within the duality of my delusion, lies both my superpower and my kryptonite: my sheer, stupid belief that I would be the exception eventually did, indeed, make me the exception.

But before I was anyone's outlier, I was just another dumb kid with a very serious dream, trying to make it in New York City. And while it might make you chuckle in equal measure to how it makes me blush, I must admit that

I thought I had my "big break" after my first-ever performance. I believed in myself so much that I thought I would have to put myself out there only *once* in order to "make it."

In my defense though, my fantasies appeared to be coming true at first.

Getting Started

I performed at the Nuyorican Poets Cafe open mic for the first time in March 2018. I had been scouting the club out for a few weeks, listening to amateur poets, musicians, and comedians and desperately praying that their courage somehow might rub off on me. I would sit at the back of the bar, in all black, hoping that people might mistake me for someone important and mysterious.

After I spent three weeks casing the joint, one of the veteran poets came over to where I was fake-sipping a beer (I had finished it thirty minutes prior) and told me it was time for me to "get up and perform or just go home." And so, the next week, I joined the ranks of someday stars, dutifully taking my place at the back of Nuyorican's infamous open mic line.

A word on the quandary of the queue: Nuyorican takes an equitable, if not cruel, approach to open mic participation. Those looking to perform begin lining up outside around 5:00 p.m. (doors don't open till 9:00 p.m.). No matter how awful the weather is, you have to guard your spot in line—rain, shine, or monstrous blizzard. It's on a first-come-first-serve basis. You're allowed to hold someone's spot in the line only if you're either already established on the scene or over six feet tall (in that case, who's gonna stop you?).

There are twenty-five spots available for performers every Monday night. Inevitably, some poor soul at the end of the line finds out that they are number twenty-six after waiting over four hours in the rain. Oh, and did I mention that the performers have to pay? Yup, ten dollars for five whole minutes of stage time. It's a brutal, beautiful system that asks the only question worth asking a fledgling artist: how bad do you want it, really?

So, on my fourth week as a New Yorker, I dutifully took my spot in the very back of the line on the Lower East Side. My secret hope was that all of those years of failing math tests would pay off and, when 9:00 p.m. rolled around, I'd be told I was Twenty-Six. Or maybe Twenty-Seven. To my dismay, I was the twentieth person in line, still five off from the cutoff. With a shaking hand, I wrote my name on the performer's list and handed over my ten bucks, too nervous to ask the MC yelling into the microphone what "on deck" meant.

Nineteen names and a good forty Hail Marys later, it was my turn to go on stage.

You're Up Next, Kid

I'm not sure what that performance was like for the audience. For me, it felt like what I can only imagine love at first sight feels like. It was that moment of "Oh, so this is what everyone was talking about" combined with the deeply grateful relief that this romance really was worth waiting for.

I finished my piece without forgetting all the words, as I had worried I would (that wouldn't happen for another two weeks), and hopped off the stage elated. The other performers congratulated me, offering me high fives that I wasn't able to return because my hands were still shaking so hard with the aftershock of adrenaline. They assured me that the hardest part was over now. Years later, I still believe this to be true: starting is so much harder than continuing or even "finishing," whatever that could possibly mean.

It takes so much more courage to perform in front of a room of twenty people for the first time than it does to perform in front of a concert hall filled with hundreds of people for the fiftieth time.

I headed to the bathroom to try to gain some composure over my vibrating palms, but before I could get there, an impossibly fashionable man hopped off his barstool and offered me his hand, noticeably without a quiver. He introduced himself as "Empress," and within minutes of meeting, I realized that he was the embodiment of the kind of person I had been hoping people would mistake me to be. A budding New York City fashion designer, he was flashy but in a fun and ironic way. Every sentence he offered me felt like an opportunity, and when he gushed over my work, I knew that my suspicions had been right all along.

I *was* the exception, wasn't I?

Sure, it takes most people years to become an overnight success, but let's call it like it is: I wasn't most people. I was the one-in-a-million, 2000s rom-com come true: the girl who moves to New York City, experiences all of her hard moments in a montage, and by the time the Nelly Furtado song is over, has overcome all adversity.

Empress told me that he was releasing a new line in a few weeks and he'd love me to perform the same poem I had performed that night at his show (which was good because, at the time, it was the only poem I had written).

I shoved my hands into my pockets, determined that my new boss wouldn't see how inexperienced I was and never suspecting that that might have been why he chose me in the first place.

The weeks passed, and I missed no opportunity to tell every friend, family member, and Dunkin' Donuts employee that after just *one* open mic, I had been booked to perform at a fashion show. Most people were supportive, and some just wanted me to pay for my doughnut and leave, but every once in a while, someone would ask a really unsupportive question, such as "Is he paying you? You said it's a fashion show, but Fashion Week was last month. You said his name is Empress? Does he have a last name?"

I responded to their pestering with more pity than annoyance. Not everyone gets to be young and in love with a dream in New York City, and even fewer get their big break after only one try. It wasn't their fault that they didn't understand. How could they possibly?

My Big Break

The day of the show arrived, and I hopped on the subway. I had enough money for only a one-way ticket, but I knew I'd be getting paid after the show, so I just hopped on the L and headed to the venue.

When I arrived, I wasn't a little bit surprised to find out that the "venue" was the second floor of a bar, which for some reason didn't strike me as odd at all. I climbed up the stairs and headed over to Empress, who embraced me with a delighted squeal. He told me that he'd show me the setup for where I'd be performing, but first, would I be a doll and help him lay out the pieces that were for sale?

To my surprise, the pieces that were for sale were actually all just T-shirts that read "EMPRESS." As per his instructions, I began marking them with little stickers: "S," "M," and "L," which looking back, I think may have stood for "So! Many! Lies!"

Guests began arriving, and I helped them fill out nametags, still unsure about when and where I was supposed to perform in this crowded bar floor filled with people taking selfies. Hours went by, and I was continually asked to help out with little administrative tasks. I wish I could say that I was upset, but truthfully, I just spent most of the night grateful for a distraction from the nerves that had my hands shaking again. See, this may surprise you, but I was nervous because I truly still believed I was going to perform that night.

It wasn't until almost midnight, when Empress came over and explicitly told me I would not be performing because "people seemed to be enjoying the DJ instead," that I understood no one would be hearing my poetry that night. Finally starting to work at a New York pace, my mind put together the fact that no performance also probably meant no payment and that perhaps—just perhaps—there had never been any plan to pay me at all.

I put on my bravest face and thanked Empress for the opportunity (to fold and label his clothes) and headed out. To my surprise though, he called out after me, laughing about how there was no way I was going to leave empty-handed after all the hard work I had put in. Generously, he handed me my payment: one XL "EMPRESS" T-shirt. I put it on, my sackcloth of shame, to show him how much I loved it and headed out to grab the L.

That's when I remembered: I had spent all my cash on the subway ticket to get to the event and didn't have enough to get home. And so, I began the very, very long walk home. You don't have to believe me about this next part, but it's true. Maybe it was just the weather or maybe God wanted to wash me clean of the awful day, but it began to rain, and I, in turn, began to cry. Shuffling home in my soaked T-shirt, I almost didn't notice when a gang of teenage boys pulled up on me on their little trick bicycles. They were about to pass right by me, but one of them must have noticed my still-shaking hands.

The leader stopped his bike and started laughing. "Look, she's crying!"

The prepubescent bats out of hell began to circle me with their bikes, and I just took off running, taking a bunch of wrong turns until I was sure I had lost them. Some time (a much longer time) later, I made it back to the 175-square-foot apartment I shared with my childhood best friend. She asked me how it went, and in between sobs and sniffles and shivers, I told her all about the tricks and the T-shirts and the evil little boys.

Somewhere around this point I grimly realized that in a way, all of my wishes had come true. I *was* one in a million . . . in a bad way. Who gets conned into a fake gig, paid in T-shirts, rained on, and mocked by children all in one day? Is this the kind of exception I was going to be? The horrific kind? The kind they make Netflix specials about?

Or was I even worse than a horror story? Was I absolutely average and completely typical, just another girl who moved to the big city thinking she had something special when I really didn't have anything different or better than anyone else?

In Retrospect

Five years have gone by, and I can now finally say with confidence that I *was* (and continue to be) absolutely average—with maybe one exception: After that awful experience, I showed back up at Nuyorican Poets Cafe that next Monday, ten dollars borrowed from my roommate in hand.

The part of the story that took the longest for me to come to terms with though is that Empress wasn't some sort of supervillain in my New York City fairy tale. No, despite how compelling and grown up I found him, Empress was actually probably only a few years older than I was at the time. And sure, he should have given me the opportunity he promised me and (ideally) paid me in paper money instead of fabric, but I can see now that he, too, was just another scared kid trying to make it in New York City, however clumsily. If I remember correctly, I later found out that he was originally from Minnesota.

Artist Moments

Are there individuals on your creative journey to whom you need to extend a little more grace and forgiveness? Use this space to release them from the blame you may be holding.

_____

_____

_____

_____

Failure Redux

I'm so grateful that I experienced my first defeat so early and so spectacularly. Many perceived "failures" were to come after this, but to be honest, most of them would pale in comparison to that first fateful day; honorable mention goes to one show I had years later: I took a four-hour bus to get to a venue where I performed for a total of three audience members (technically there were six, but three were on their phones).

I'd also be remiss if I didn't give a nod to the inevitable day when I'd quit my day job to pursue poetry full time, putting my faith and future in all of the shows I had lined up around the country, only to have them all canceled because of a new virus that seemed to have taken hold in Seattle.

The funny thing though is that when those arguably much more devastating defeats came, *they didn't rattle me the way that first one did.* As I said, the starting is so much harder than the continuing. By the time the big blows came,

I was much more prepared to fight back, this time without the shaking hands.

Artist MOMENTS

What are some opportunities within your art-making practice in which you can practice the perseverance-adjacent virtue of tenacity?

_____

_____

_____

_____

_____

_____

_____

_____

_____

_____

_____

Waiting on Resurrection

It is so important for young artists to be encouraged to "fail" early, often, and hard.

When we first start out, we have something going for us that is easy to overlook: there will never be a lower-risk time in our lives to fall on our faces. As we age, our responsibilities grow and thus, an understandable aversion to risk grows with them. At twenty-three, I could afford to learn hard lessons at a "huge" personal cost because the only thing I had to lose was my pride.

In our youth, we have a bouncy ball quality to us, so when someone hurls us to the ground, we just bounce back up and maybe even light up a little (if the battery pack still works). But the longer we go without throwing ourselves face first at the ground, the more brittle we become and the higher our fear of shattering on impact becomes.

The ability to fail well is a use-it-or-lose-it skill. The earlier we can get our big blunders out of the way, the better we'll be able to understand how to navigate them. This truth is proven over and over through the Gospel, most notably in the Passion story. While Christ never failed, his Crucifixion was a perceived and celebrated failure by his enemies. But his story was one of Resurrection, just as ours will be if we can only summon the courage.

Artist MOMENTS

What if we reframed our failures as only "perceived failures"? What if we saw life's many crucifixions as the foreshadowing of great resurrections?

_____

_____

_____

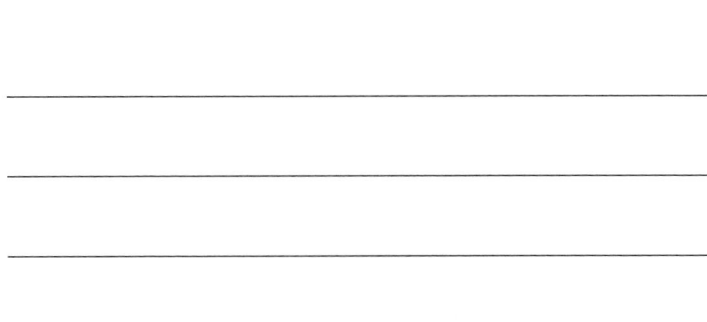

The Way of the Cross for the Artist

As both artists and Christians, crucifixion and resurrection are written into our story from the start. There's a great opportunity in this though, as it echoes the story of our Savior. It wasn't until I united my journey to his that I came to accept suffering and resurrection as a privilege rather than something I feel victimized by. Through the Passion, I finally came to find solace in the knowledge that defeat is never real or permanent when I'm walking in God's will.

When I started, delusion was my greatest strength; if I had known how painful the defeats would be, I don't know that I would have held on long enough to get to the resurrections. These days, however, truth is my superpower. Rooting myself in truth instead of blissful ignorance has given me a much firmer foundation because *truth* is from God. Delusion helped me bounce back from tough breaks, but truth, however more difficult a weight to carry, has allowed me to see my defeats as gift rather than "just having to pay my dues." As an artist and as an individual, I would be nothing without the heartbreaks that have united me to the ultimate artist, my Creator.

Interview with an Artist:
ON WHAT SUCCESS IS—AND ISN'T
with Luisamaria Hernandez

One friend who has helped me learn to trust in God's truth above all else is Luisamaria Hernandez, an opera singer, storyteller, and producer. I'm lucky enough to spend almost every day with her, but I wanted to make sure that you have the opportunity to meet her and hear about the roles doubt and confidence have played in her journey.

"I have always felt that creating for God was what I am called to do," Luisamaria said to me. "Since it's of him and for him, I never doubted that success would come. Maybe I'm not at the point of traditional [financial] success that people imagine. But God has given me confidence that I have a pretty clear idea of what it is that he wants me to do with the gifts that he's giving me. That fuels the feeling that I've made it somehow."

One of the things I most admire about my friend is the way she responds to closed doors and unanswered prayers. She seems to let those losses roll right off her in a way that I still haven't quite managed to do, so I had to ask her how she does it.

> Life can be challenging, but it's worth it to do beautiful things for God. If I were doing these things for me—for the way they make me feel, for the way they make me look—then I'm sure the difficulties would multiply exponentially. When I was in middle school, I once heard Michael Jordan say that every time you get rejected, it brings you closer to the time you'll be accepted. That has become the way that I look at opportunities. God has a really good plan for me, but I can say with complete confidence that any opportunity that has somehow not worked out was because it wasn't in the plan that he had written for me.

Reflection QUESTIONS

- » What would you consider your most spectacular failure as an artist?
- » How did you respond to failure back then? How do you respond to it now?
- » Do you consider yourself "the exception"? Do you expect things to come easily to you? Why?
- » What is the value of failure?
- » If fear of failure is holding you back from expressing yourself creatively, how can you overcome that fear?

Chapter 7

CREATING WITH YOUR CROSS

(How Creativity Can Be a Source of Healing)

> Be gracious to me, O Lord, for I am languishing; O Lord, heal me, for my bones are shaking with terror.
>
> —Psalm 6:2

I have a complicated relationship with some of the most painful days of my life. While I'd give anything to be able to fill in these craters in my heart, I really don't think I'd be much of a writer if I had never suffered what my friend Teresa Pitt Green describes as "bone marrow–level agony."

Ironically, some of my greatest losses have been things that I never really had in the first place. Most of us at one time in our lives will experience the acute pain of losing someone or something you once held dear, especially a loved one. And yet, as I've gotten older, I've discovered a different, yet surprisingly common, kind of grief: crying over something I've never had. It's more like a permanent ache in the bones (or "bone marrow," as Teresa calls it) than a gash in the skin or a bruise on the knees. It's chronic and it's cruel, lying dormant just long enough to delude myself into thinking it's gone for good this time.

And it is in accepting its permanence that we can find the true gift of this kind of pain: if you're forever close to the Cross, then you're forever close to Christ as well.

It was this kind of loss that drove me to write in the first place. In naming my pain, I was forced to confront my many underlying aches—wounds that I had just excused as "part of me." And though total healing is still a long way off, through writing I found something just as important: strength to face the reality of my situation, to work through it, and to eventually move on in whatever way I could.

Strength in Weakness

In my senior year of college, I experienced the sudden, tragic loss of a family member.

It may seem trite, but the only way I've ever been able to describe my reaction to the news was that I "lost my marbles." Something about the imagery of watching my mind spill out and roll away from me so perfectly fits what actually happened that I've never been able to bring myself to find a more flowery way to describe it.

There's so much of that year that I genuinely just don't remember. People tell me stories about parties I attended or memories we made, and I don't remember any of it. My body was there, but my mind was still rolling away from me . . . and I didn't even have it in me to run after it.

Writing was what allowed me to begin to pick those little glass pieces back up and place them where they belonged, fashioning a kind of life mosaic. My technical skills were nonexistent, and to be honest, I'm not even convinced that I started with any particular talent. But what I had at that time, perhaps more than I've had any time since, was pain . . . and I desperately wanted others to see and acknowledge that pain. I guess I thought that somehow, in seeing and acknowledging my suffering, they would be able to alleviate it with their gaze alone.

As I reread my blog and social media posts from that time, they paint a very clear portrait of a suffering young woman trying to make sense of lost innocence in a very public way. I kept showing my wounds to strangers on the internet instead of showing them to Christ, as if the pity in their eyes or the praise in their comments could heal me.

I put my faith in self-expression. And it failed me.

I didn't make any real breakthroughs in healing until I finally went to Confession with a priest on campus. I had a *lot* to confess—least of all a red-hot anger at God for allowing me to experience this loss. We sat face-to-face, and I told him what had happened over the last year. Our conversation lasted over an hour and ended with both of us crying and embracing after the priest told me that he, too, had lost someone in a similarly tragic way at my age. For the first time, I had gone past reckless catharsis and told my story to the right person.

And while it may have looked as if the person I was telling my story to was the priest hearing my confession, it was a direct communication with God through the sacrament that brought me peace. When the priest told me that he had suffered the same way I had, it was truly Christ showing me that every pain I had felt, he had felt too.

When I started writing, all I had was an understanding of pain, which isn't an awful place to start, but it would be an awful place to stop. But through the grace of the sacraments, I received the gift that I needed in order to become a true artist: an understanding of the Cross.

Artist MOMENTS

For whom do you create? Who are you hoping sees you and your cross through your work?

_____

_____

_____

_____

_____

_____

_____

_____

_____

_____

_____

_____

The Cross, the Paintbrush, and the Pen

For artists, the Cross isn't simply a symbol of sacrifice but rather a commission. The crucifix isn't a piece of home décor; it's an invitation to join him in a place of pain and humiliation, for the absolute love of our neighbor. He summons artists, in particular, to sacrifice themselves and their own stories in a way that will bring people to him through beauty.

When I meditate on this, I imagine my pen and paintbrush being carved from the wood of his Cross. As I imagine myself creating with the splinters of the altar on which he was sacrificed, the work I create takes on new weight and I have no choice but to hold my own words to a higher standard.

For the artist who so often has to wrestle with pride and ambition, the invitation to join Christ in a place of humiliation is curious and even a bit chilling. Most of us who create, whether we'd like to admit it or not, indulge in the occasional fantasy that our work may someday become successful by worldly standards, bringing us money and fame and thus definitive validation. Luckily though, it's easy to get a reality check for these delusions: Ask anyone you know whose creative work has won them the type of wealth and fame you aspire to whether they have found peace in their accomplishments. Invariably, the answer will be no. And if they're feeling particularly honest, they might even tell you that the more weight that external validation takes in their life, the more insecure they feel.

However, if you were to do the inverse and ask someone who radiates peace where they get their security from, I bet their answer, whether they realize it or not, will call the mind this scripture passage:

> And not only that, but we also boast in our sufferings, knowing that suffering produces endurance, and endurance produces character, and character produces hope, and hope does not disappoint us, because God's love has been poured into our hearts through the Holy Spirit that has been given to us. (Rom 5:3–5)

To embody this verse is to truly have a relationship with redemptive suffering and thus Christ on the Cross. My friend Teresa, the same one who taught me about the type of agony you feel in your bones, embodies this verse perhaps better than anyone I know. I visited her at Enders Island, the Catholic community focused on beauty and healing where she lives and works, to learn more from her.

Interview with an Artist:
ON ENDERS ISLAND
with Teresa Pitt Green

As we sat in one of the dining rooms at Enders Island, sipping tea and sharing stories, I became overwhelmed by the journeys that had brought us together. For me, getting to know Teresa feels like getting to know myself—or at least, who I might be capable of becoming someday if I really buckle down.

 Teresa is a writer, speaker, and advocate for trauma-informed care for abuse, especially within the Church. She spent much of her career leading an organization she cofounded called "Spirit Fire," which brings restorative justice to those wounded by abuse within the Church. These days, she lives on the island and serves as a spiritual counselor to retreatants, including the young men in the island's recovery program.

A survivor herself, Teresa is one of those rare people who chooses not just to carry her own cross but also to take on others'. Something about watching her elect to bear the weight of so much suffering, instead of running from it, brings out both the Veronica and the Simon of Cyrene in me. The brave part of me is inspired to offer help, to ask what it would take to become just like her someday—but the cowardly part of me is too afraid to even consider what it would take to become just like her. And so, paralyzed by my own weakness, I just took on the posture of the women at the foot of the Cross, holding back tears as my friend told me her story.

For three hours, Teresa and I talked about what it really means to help someone carry their cross and how sacred art can bring resurrection into the recovery process. In a quiet moment between our bursts of conversation, she remarked that she would just as soon never tell her story again, but she knows that it's what allows other survivors to feel comfortable with her, enough so that she can help them. Her willingness to share her own story was deeply humbling; I felt I was being entrusted with something precious and delicate. "Lord," I prayed, "make me worthy to receive such a gift."

Between the ages of six and nineteen, Teresa was abused by six different priests. Since then, she has left and returned to the Church countless times, attended over five thousand hours of therapy, and been in Al-Anon for thirty-nine years. So many people would spend their entire lives running away from that kind of pain, and who could blame them? Instead, Teresa has redeemed her pain by making her story a source of healing to the wounds of others. Part of that entails helping fellow survivors find themselves in the Crucifixion and Resurrection. As she reminded me, even after he rose from the dead, he still had wounds, not scars.

My breath caught as I remembered the post-Resurrection encounter of Jesus and Thomas, when Jesus said, "Reach out your hand and put it in my side" (Jn 20:27).

She was right. "He still had wounds, not scars."

I have to admit that, even after twelve years of Catholic schooling under my belt, I had never before thought about this. I had always assumed that when God heals someone, all evidence of what had happened disappeared entirely. I was dismayed to discover I was wrong.

My face must have given me away because, with a gentle smile, she asked, "In the new life that God is going to give you, how will your wounds be part of your resurrection and identity?"

Unsure how to answer a question I had never even considered asking myself before, I changed the subject, asking her to tell me more about the connection between sacred art and recovery. I think she saw right through me, but she graciously went along with my scattered line of questioning.

"Sacred art is art that represents the true, beautiful, and good—and it usually reflects something of God and something of faith," she told me. "Anyone can make it, but I associate it with a master and a student. I associate it as a relational experience and a sharing of not just history but also faith. It's prayerful. It's mysterious. And I think that if we say we want to draw or create something in his honor, he won't abandon us in that process."

Had God ever pursued her through beauty? She paused and took a sip of her tea before beginning her story. In New

York City in 1985, she was fleeing the snow and ran into the Church of St. Francis of Assisi on 31st Street. In the main church, she was overwhelmed by the big, bright space and sought refuge in the basement chapel, where unbeknownst to her, adoration was about to begin. In the candlelight of the lower chapel, she saw an image of St. Anthony holding Jesus and felt immediately infuriated: "Don't they know there's a sex abuse scandal in a church? And here's a friar holding a baby in the church?"

In her head, she began to plan the letter she would write to the archdiocese, but then benediction started and she was completely overcome by the beauty of the Eucharist. She told me that she sees that as the turning point that brought her home and that in her, "St. Anthony found something that was lost."

While her return to faith began that day, the healing process was far from linear. Five years later, at age thirty, she developed a series of brain tumors due to increased cortisol from the abuse. Bedridden during treatment, she would stare at the portrait of St. Thérèse hanging across from her bed, the same one that comforted her in her family's home as a little girl. St. Thérèse would just stare back at her, and she thought about what she had always told others about sacred art: sacred art is art that "doesn't abandon us." In that moment, she was drawn to consider how Christ had accompanied her through beauty throughout her most difficult trials.

Teresa, Teresa, and Thérèse

No sooner had my friend Teresa told me about her sacred art encounter with Thérèse when she reminded me of St.

Teresa of Avila's famous quip to Christ: "If this is how You treat Your friends, no wonder why You have so few of them!"

St. Teresa, not unlike my friend Teresa, was a reformer. And, as Teresa Pitt Green reminded me, reformation starts not externally but internally, within the individual. "If you want to help people who have been traumatized, you have to go deep within yourself and deal with all the wounds you carry. If you want to be a Christian these days, you have to dig deep."

When I pressed her further about the relationship between healing trauma and sacred art, she told me, "All trauma is relational, and in being relational, all trauma is spoken. An abuser is full of lies. So, what do you believe? What can you trust? Jesus, who will never lie."

When she said this, I couldn't help but recall my own experience of tending to my wounds through writing. My instinct had been so close to the truth and yet still disordered. Something within me had known that trauma and healing are relational, and that art has the power to heal, but I had sought that healing relationship with random audiences instead of the one person who actually had the power to bring me peace. Perhaps, in my pain, I hadn't even thought to seek healing and instead settled for the quick fix of attention and affirmation.

If I could, I would tell my younger self that if you create for Christ alone, in a relational way, then any audience that comes after that will be natural, healthy, and right. Carrying a cross is a universal experience; if we accept our crosses as commission, then the work we create will always have that relational aspect that makes sacred art so uniquely powerful.

There is a prayer, attributed to St. Teresa of Avila, that encompasses what it truly means to see your cross as commission:

> Christ has no body but yours,
> No hands, no feet on earth but yours,
> Yours are the eyes with which He looks
> Compassion on this world.

Christ has no paintbrush but ours, no pen but ours, no voice to sing out songs of mercy and resurrection but ours. If we, as artists, have the courage to celebrate our suffering as an opportunity to partake in not only the Crucifixion but also the Resurrection, imagine the healing we can bring to both ourselves and others.

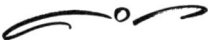

Reflection QUESTIONS

- » Is my art catharsis or confessional . . . or something else?
- » How can I witness to my wounds without succumbing to them?
- » Do I find healing through my creative process? How do I seek resurrection through my art?
- » In whose art do I find healing?

Chapter 8

LABOR TOWARD NEW LIFE

(Experiencing the Creative Process as a Form of Parenthood)

> To be a mother is to nourish and protect true humanity and bring it to development.
> —Edith Stein

My cousin Kelli is one of my best friends. We're complete opposites in most ways, but there's a deep tie—familial and feminine—that I believe will hold us together for the rest of our lives. In the last three years, Kelli has gotten married and had *three* beautiful baby girls, while I have continued my twenty-nine-year run as our Irish Catholic family's token "artsy city girl who can't keep a boyfriend for the life of her." Our paths have been so distinct that you might assume they never run parallel, but to both of our surprise, her maternity has actually matched strides with my creative journey.

It's simple but sweet: no matter what our vocation may be, God designed his children to look like him. Any prolific nature we find within ourselves is just as patrimonial as blue eyes or attached earlobes. As artists, our gifts and creative inclinations are our birthright, gifts from our Father—gifts that make us look and act like him.

Perhaps no one has ever understood this in such a holistic way as St. John Paul II. In his 1999 *Letter to Artists*, he wrote:

> Through his "artistic creativity" man appears more than ever "in the image of God," and he accomplishes this task above all in shaping the wondrous "material" of his own humanity and then exercising creative dominion over the universe which surrounds him. With loving regard, the divine Artist passes on to the human artist a spark of his own surpassing wisdom, calling him to share in his creative power.[1]

The connection between his words on art and his teachings on the "Theology of the Body" (1979–1984) was foreshadowed on a retreat he gave in Krakow in 1962, which all but disappeared from public record until it was published in Polish in 2011, and finally in English in a book entitled *God Is Beauty: A Retreat on the Gospel and Art*. In his initial reflection, he quotes the Polish poet Zygmunt Krasiński: "A stream of Beauty flows through you, but you yourself are not Beauty."

As with any man or a woman who hopes to conceive a child, we cannot create entirely on our own. Even at the height of our talent, all we ever are is a co-creator. We should take this truth as encouragement rather than discouragement. Since we can create beautiful work only in cooperation with Beauty himself, we are guaranteed that the work we create will be beautiful. Isn't that an honor?

So, practically speaking, how can we live out the marriage of Theology of the Body and *Letter to Artists*, in order to embody John Paul II's teaching on art-making as creative motherhood and fatherhood? Both parents and artists experience similar stages of creative development.

Romance

Before new life can be brought forth—or even conceived—the romance begins and ideally culminates in marriage. The young artist experiences a similar brush with romance the first time they encounter beauty. Whether it be in the theater, a museum, a concert hall, or even the pages of a book, we are struck by the arrow of beauty and captivated by it entirely. For many, this begins a lifelong devotion to art, as either a creator or a consumer—or hopefully both.

Like lovers, artists blaze past the blinking yellow lights of infatuation and speed over the rumble strips of self-doubt before crashing joyfully down the cliff of self-abandonment to their beloved. And like lovers, they aspire to a mutual sense of reciprocal (or close to it) giving and receiving. Beauty and creation serve them, filling their soul with wonder and purpose while leading them to truth and goodness. And in return, they serve beauty through their tireless devotion; their sleepless nights, calloused hands, splitting headaches, and paint-splattered jeans all bundle together to become a bouquet left at Beauty's doorstep.

St. Thomas Aquinas wrote, "To love is to will the good of another." His wisdom contained so much truth that it was even put in the *Catechism of the Catholic Church* (*CCC* 1766). In my life, I've often heard his statement paraphrased and extrapolated even further: to love is to will the good of another, *even above your own*.

A lover abandons cheap pleasure and instant gratification and instead sacrifices for and invests in their beloved. Marriage is the ultimate example of this unselfish, holy kind of fidelity. Abandoning all logic or sense of self-preservation, the enraptured lover, knee to the floor, humbles themselves and asks for the privilege of putting their beloved before them, for the rest of their lives. I recently found a journal entry from my early twenties, right after I had truly fallen in love with writing poetry, that truly expresses this desperate desire to become worthy of my beloved:

> "An idea started yesterday while I was rocking a screaming baby and finished today while I was cleaning dog poop off the sidewalk."
>
> I love my art best when I do the things that, on the surface, have the least to do with my art. I fight for my art best when I'm doing the things that have the least to do with my art. Which is a necessity because my art can't be romanced the way most others can. And why should she be? She is a New York woman, after all. If you don't believe me, try reciting a poem to Poetry herself and tell me how far it gets you. I guarantee you'll never see a second date, let alone the life you've been dreaming of.
>
> No, it seems the only thing that can woo her is feet-aching, back-twisting hard work. She told me in no uncertain terms: She isn't interested in another starving artist. She wants stability. She wants security. She wants someone worth committing to. She's the lady, not easily impressed. And I'm her unfortunate suitor, not hardly discouraged.
>
> And tonight, much to her bemusement, she spotted me walking home from another odd job and uneven paycheck. She called for her sisters to rise from

bed and see the poor sucker who's been throwing rocks at her window these last few years. Even at my expense, her humor enticed me.

    Poetry must have been feeling particularly devilish, and I must have been feeling particularly gullible, because when she sat on the sill and asked how I planned on making a life for her, I answered in earnest. I shouted back about the dog walking and babysitting. I shouted back that all you actually really need is love. I shouted back even after she closed the window, collapsing into giggles at another lovesick fool.

Now years removed from the writing of this piece, I smile, knowing that I really did give everything to my beloved and it gave me absolutely *everything* in return: a home at the artists' home, my community of creators, the chance to see the world, and the opportunity to write this book. As I suspected it would be, even all that time ago, the great romance of self-abandonment to my art was worth every sacrifice.

Conception

> Before I formed you in the womb I knew you,
> And before you were born I consecrated you;
> I have appointed you a prophet to the nations.
> —Jeremiah 1:5

After romance and union comes conception—and the biological process we call *conception* can be understood in our creative life as divine inspiration. The intimacy of conception extends to creative commission as well. When God asks us to write, paint, or sing something that reflects him, we are entering into a relationship even more personal than the physical relationship needed to conceive!

Isn't that absolutely amazing? Isn't it humbling?

Henri Nouwen illustrates this point in his book *Clowning in Rome*, describing the sculptor as co-creator with his marble:

> The art of sculpture is, first of all, the art of seeing. In one block of marble, Michelangelo saw a loving mother holding her dead son on her lap, while in another, he saw a self-confident David ready to hurl his stone at the approaching Goliath, and in a third, he saw an irate Moses at the point of rising in anger from his seat. Visual art is indeed the art of seeing, and the practice of disciplines is a way to make visible what has been seen. The skillful artist is a liberator who frees from bondage the figures hidden for billions of years inside the marble. The artist reveals the true identity of the figures![2]

As Nouwen suggests, we can "free from bondage" the image of Christ within us and release it back into the world. To receive creative inspiration from God is to begin that carving, to conceive.

Gestation

After the conception—the union between Creator and craftsman—comes the gestation. Like a physical pregnancy, carrying an idea within yourself is equal parts beautiful, exciting, and exhausting. As it grows within you, inspiration can grow heavy; and the carrier, weary. As a mother sacrifices her body and her autonomy for the child she carries, the artist makes heroic sacrifices to create something

Labor toward New Life

beautiful, true, and good. St. John Paul II referred to this sacrifice in his 1962 address, saying:

> How many hours are spent pounding on the piano keys or seeking the right sounds on some other instrument? . . . This incorporation of beauty in a work of art, this search for means of expression in every artist's craft, in every artist's work—it costs so much. One pays so much for talent! For vocal talent, for physical talent. How many attempts are needed to draw out a different theatrical character from one's own concrete, unequivocal character, to create—from the person that I am—another person.[3]

His next comment draws a breathtaking parallel between artistry and parenthood: "What a huge transfer of my individuality, personality; what a huge plasticity of all of the dispositions of my person is required so that in its place, a different 'I' arises—authentic and original."[4]

Sound familiar? Like motherhood? Like fatherhood? Like creating something that is somehow a direct reflection of you and yet also completely sovereign and distinct?

Beauty is only something that flows through us; we can't hold our creations within us forever, even though we might fear the pains of birthing them into the world.

But once the creation is fully formed, it is time to push.

Labor

John Paul II is unrelenting in his conviction on the connection between maternity and creativity. He explicitly connects creative pains and labor pains, warning artists that they will have to pay for talent but also promising them it will be worth it. What John Paul II refers to as the "pain of creation" we can understand as labor pains. These creative labor pains can be understood as a sort of voluntary crucifixion toward the larger goal of resurrection in not only our spirits but also our art.

How validating is it to hear St. John Paul II affirm what so many of us have felt confused about and perhaps even shame over: the fact that creating beautiful art is *painful*. For years, I have wrestled with guilt over the way I avoid creating in order to avoid pain. The sheer effort alone is often enough to keep me from beginning a project.

Birth is beautiful, not despite its violence but because of it. It is the tearing of flesh and the pouring of blood that makes childbearing a crucifixion and thus sacred. As Christ gave his body on the Cross, a mother sacrifices her body for her child.

Artists have to die to themselves in order to deliver their creations into the world. Artists die to their pride, to their peace of mind, and to their sense of control.

Artist MOMENTS

What does the pain of creation feel like to you? Is it exhausting? Overwhelming? Does it carry a sense of unfulfilled longing? Consider using this space to understand that pain through poetry.

_____

_____

_____

Holding Your Creation

The most painful "little death" is dying to one's sense of control. The pain this inflicts is most acute after your creation has been born into the world and other people ask to hold it. To trust your creation—the most precious reflection of yourself and your relationship with the divine—to such a dangerous and cruel world is to be in a constant, simmering state of fear.

It is up to the artist to balance a sense of detachment with their urge to protect what they've created. The instinct to shield our creations from detractors can be even more dangerous than any misunderstanding or mockery of our work. As mere vessels of beauty and not authors of beauty, hoarding it would be a much greater failure than sharing it in an imperfect way. There's a sense of humility and trust that we must embody to have a healthy relationship with our work after we've shared it with the world.

Inscribed on the walls of the Missionaries of Charity mission house in Calcutta, there is a poem that reads:

> People are often unreasonable, illogical and self-centered;
> Forgive them anyway.
> If you are kind, people may accuse you of selfish, ulterior motives;
> Be kind anyway.
> If you are successful, you will win some false friends and some true enemies;
> Succeed anyway.
> If you are honest and frank, people may cheat you;
> Be honest and frank anyway.
> What you spend years building, someone could destroy overnight;
> Build anyway.
> If you find serenity and happiness, they may be jealous;
> Be happy anyway.
> The good you do today, people will often forget tomorrow;
> Do good anyway.
> Give the world the best you have, and it may never be enough;
> Give the world the best you've got anyway.
> You see, in the final analysis, it is between you and your God;
> It was never between you and them anyway.

The founder of the Missionaries of Charity, Mother Teresa, knew a thing or two about maternity. This beautiful prayer can and should be applied to prolific art-making—there may be those who aren't worthy of your vulnerability, but you should offer them Beauty anyway. Creating is an act of love, and there is no fear in love, only trust in God and the path he has set before us.

Interview with an Artist:
BECOMING A SHELTER
with Karina Breceda

When I think of maternity and creativity, one friend comes to mind before all others. Karina Breceda is the creator and leader of an artist collective based in Ciudad Juárez, Mexico, called Haznos Valer. The collective seeks to bring attention, through art, to the plight of the migrants on the Texas/Mexico border. Karina is also the founder and leader of two shelters for women and children—one on the Texas side and the other on the Mexico side. Her shelters are unique as they specifically offer resources that pregnant women and mothers might need during their migration journey and arrival to a new and unfamiliar country. Karina is also a mother of three children who admire and adore their mother just as much as I do.

Labor toward New Life

I recently visited Karina to see the shelters in person and begin to plan how we'll integrate artists into her work at the border even more going forward. Ideally, our plan is to bring artists in residence to the shelters so they can use their gifts to bring beauty to places that can otherwise feel very transient and cold. Sitting together, dreaming and scheming with one of my very best friends, I couldn't help but feel the old familiar kicks in my womb. The idea we had conceived over the many late-night voice notes that had traveled between us was now growing heavy within us, preparing to enter the world with a loud and glorious cry.

As we entered into this time of creative maternity together, I asked Karina to tell me about the parallels between labor, delivery, and motherhood in her life as both a parent and a creative. She replied, "Motherhood brings out my desire to sacrifice and withstand discomfort. My good stuff comes from when I'm having a hard time."

I asked her which part of both physical and creative pregnancy she found the hardest, suspecting that as with many women, she would say labor. However, she told me that she enjoys the "relief of the final push" and that actually, "the hardest part is the monotony of the carrying."

Her phrasing struck me. Had I ever experienced the monotony of carrying? Of course I had. I recalled my old journal entries, the odes written to my art and the excitement of new love. But those journal entries lose meaning entirely when I forget that pages later, I was writing about the absolute exhaustion of the pursuit. By the time I ran out of pages and needed my next notebook, not only had I won over my love, but also I was finally bearing its fruit. As it did for Karina, the carrying of the lineage of my great love felt not just endless but a bit scary too—almost . . . isolating. I wondered aloud why that might be, and Karina responded with an answer that struck me.

"As both a mother and an artist, society isn't set up for you. Both roles are isolating." Both mothers and artists tend to be all but invisible in society, despite their heroic and necessary contributions. And so, I had to ask her, Why does she do it anyway if a good half of it feels like discomfort and there's barely any acknowledgement at all?

"I'm trying to create what I didn't have, for my children. And people don't see the power behind being a mother or an artist, and there's power in that."

I agree with my friend—maybe some of the magic of maternity comes from the humility of it. As romance is fueled only by vulnerability and birth is bought only through pain, maybe beauty finds its power in humility.

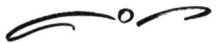

Reflection QUESTIONS

» How do you feel about being a co-creator with God? What does a moment of divine creative inspiration feel like in your body? What does it feel like in your soul?
» How does it feel to carry an idea inside of you as it grows? How do you know it's time to start pushing?
» Do the words of St. John Paul II—that one pays for talent—resonate with you? What has it cost you? Has it been worth it?
» Do you ever fear that others won't respect or understand your creation once it's out in the world?

Chapter 9

THEATER KIDS WILL INHERIT THE WORLD

(Creating a Community of Sustaining and *Sustainable* Relationships)

> We are each other's harvest; we are each other's business;
> we are each other's magnitude and bond.
> —Gwendolyn Brooks

Over the next few years, our program would undergo many exciting and often painful changes. As the creative director, I quickly discovered that my leadership style could be summarized: "Learn the hard way." If those first few months could be measured in Home Depot visits, the first few years can be measured in the number of times I had to apologize for my many failings as a well-intentioned but more-often-wrong-than-right leader.

One of the most brutal examples that comes to mind is an ill-fated house meeting I called after a lackluster open mic night. Attendance had been low and the performances, I felt, uninspiring. I was frustrated because I felt as if our artists in residence hadn't been practicing and it showed in their performances.

To be fair, I was right. To be even fairer, I handled it horribly. However constructively I may have intended my criticism, that wasn't the way anyone received it. By the time I was done, all of the artists were crying.

I left the meeting baffled. All I had done was tell them the truth, and as I kept saying to anyone who would listen, they knew they hadn't been putting in the time and that it was showing in their work. Why hadn't they been able to receive my criticism as leadership or even just fraternal correction?

Nevertheless, I apologized to each person individually the next day, not necessarily out of guilt but more so out of obligation. It would be another *year* before I understood what I had done wrong.

What Makes a Bad Mentor?

As time went on, God gave me opportunities to grow. And in a way, that is just so *him*; those opportunities were always painful and often a little embarrassing. As my career progressed, mentors started reaching out and offering to nurture what they saw in me.

Humbled, I accepted and started meeting with a few different women whose journeys I admired. But to my horror, more than one of these situations ended with them exploding at me over my mistakes. The failings that they took issue with weren't unethical or even lazy—they were simply reflections of my inexperience. I didn't know what I didn't know, and I needed someone to explain my errors to me with grace and patience.

I left those relationships feeling embarrassed and cynical, telling myself that this is what happens when you meet your heroes. I convinced myself that because those mentors had been unkind in their corrections, their advice must not have any merit.

After so many experiences that weren't constructive, it was a while before I was able to accept even the most graceful guidance. Finally, a Catholic author named Shannon Evans took me under her wing, becoming both my friend and my editor at the *National Catholic Reporter*. After a few months of working under Shannon, she sent me a note accompanying her latest round of edits on a recent piece I wrote:

> [I] wanted to let you know that it's awesome and you're killing these things. And because of that I am getting a little more picky because I think you're ready for that and you'll grow into it so well. You are so talented and have so much to say and I selfishly want to help you become a great, not just a good, writer! So don't freak out when I edit a lot. It's because you're the real deal.

This note accompanied 117 of the most thoughtful and helpful edits I had ever received.

One hundred. And. Seventeen.

But because she had crafted her edits as an investment in my work, I wasn't embarrassed or resentful. I was grateful. Her note made it clear that she was going to stick with me through the painful process of becoming a better writer. Her friendship gave me the courage to keep kicking, and soon I realized I wasn't drowning in red ink—I was learning to swim in it. Through her gentle guidance, I was able to learn from my mistakes, experiencing a kind of restoration and growth through this painful process.

Artist MOMENTS

Do you have a mentor? Could your practice benefit from one? Use this space to create a list of people you might consider asking to mentor you in your creative work and the qualities you would like to emulate.

_____

_____

_____

_____

_____

_____

_____

_____

_____

Shannon's example also reminded me of my early failings at that house meeting and challenged me to take ownership of my shortcomings as a leader. When I had confronted my artists in residence over what I perceived as lack of effort, I had prioritized my critiques over my relationships. I hadn't communicated any investment in these people, only disdain. This truth was difficult to swallow because it necessitated my accepting that I had, however inadvertently, broken the sense of trust I had been working so hard to build.

As I thought about what had happened, I recalled a verse St. Paul wrote to the church at Galatia about restoring relationships damaged by sin: "My friends, if anyone is detected in a transgression, you who have received the Spirit should restore such a one in a spirit of gentleness. Take care that you yourselves are not tempted" (Gal 6:1).

How often do I forget to craft my corrections as restoration? Shannon prioritized fraternity before correction, so her edits brought restoration not only to my work but also to me as an artist. She didn't belittle me but rather chose to *invest* in me and help me become a better writer. In this way, she elevated editing to kingdom building.

Restoration and Construction

In building St. Joseph's Home for Artisans, our courageous little group of aspiring artists worked hard to achieve an important goal: to become not just artists but artists *in community*. As we tore down the wallpaper and emptied out the rotting furniture, we were building a home, an ultimate safe space, and a place where self-expression would turn into something even more important: an invitation to express Christ's presence within them. And that takes a mighty sort of courage.

I made so many mistakes in building this home. I have been unkind, prideful, selfish, and lazy—and that's just on any given Tuesday. So many of the artists who have come through our space have, at one time or another, become casualties of my learning curve, and that's something I deeply regret. Our fall artists always inherit a better home and experience than our summer artists, and our winter artists receive something even better than those fall artists—because our community is committed to growth, no matter how painful and humbling.

As for me, I am hoping to become a leader like Shannon.

Why Do We Need Each Other?

When I look back at my experiences as both the creative director of the artists' home and the lucky recipient of Shannon's creative direction, it becomes very clear to me how badly we as artists need each other.

Though we do it imperfectly, our efforts to encourage each other are crucial. I now understand kingdom building to be less like melting clouds into a swirling marble staircase and more like the day we moved into St. Joseph's home, mold spray and all. There is a lot of junk and pollution we have to help each other clear out, not only as artists but also as Christians, before we can start building the good stuff. We do this through critiquing each other's work and by collaborating, offering accountability, and always telling the truth with kindness and clarity.

While so much of our practice as Christian artists is usually focused on sharing beauty to direct others to truth, creating in community requires us to use plain truth to help each other embody and reflect beauty. Those moments of honesty with ourselves and others might be painful, but they're worth every moment of discomfort.

Interview with an Artist:
REAPING THE HARVEST
with Molly Broekman

In the first chapter, I interviewed our first-ever resident at St. Joseph's Home for Artisans, so it seems only right to conclude the final chapter with an interview with the most recent artist to come through our door, Molly Broekman. Molly is the very definition of a multi-hyphenate. She came to us as an enormously talented clothing designer, but in the two months since she joined us, she's blossomed into a prolific painter and even started writing and performing her own original music. As I write this in my living room right now, she's standing on a stepladder and painting a mural of the Sacred Heart on the ceiling while singing to herself, softly and beautifully.

In many ways, Molly and her experience at St. Joseph's are the long-awaited fruit of the seeds that we planted all those years ago. What we saw as simply cleaning out dust-filled bedrooms and tearing down peeling wallpaper was actually the creation of a clean, bright canvas for Molly and her fellow artists to create on. Watching her paint breathtaking images of Our Lady on the walls we once scrubbed mold from feels like a prayer answered and a promise kept.

I asked Molly if she would be my final artist interview, and she balked, "Are you sure you want to interview *me*?" Paintbrush in hand, she looked me in the eyes and said, in all seriousness, "I'm not really an artist. I just like to make things."

I laughed and told her that yes, I'd really like to interview *her*. I asked her more about that old mental block against calling herself an artist, and she insisted that she really sees herself more as a paintbrush than a painter, telling me that she feels more comfortable referring to herself as a "maker" than anything else. I talked to her a little bit more about being a co-creator, and that brought us back to the topic of collaborative community.

She told me, "I had absolutely no faith community at all for years and I went to a commuter school, so even though I was supposedly surrounded by other creatives, I didn't really interact with them much. I was in school during the pandemic too, so I went from having very little interaction to no interaction at all."

After graduation, she took a job as an art teacher but found that it was depleting all her creative energy. Needing a chance to just go create art on her own, she applied to St. Joe's and joined us in June.

> Living in creative community has been amazing. I had never lived away from my family. I love my family, but it's been really nice to be able to figure out who I am without them as my base. Being here has been like having a blank canvas and figuring out how I'm going to fill it in. I've felt so much freedom to make. I feel like, when I have space to breathe, I'm a lot more creative than I thought I was. When I'm back home, I have to go searching for inspiration. Here it just comes naturally.

Hearing her say these words gave me a certain feeling of healing. Seeing Molly reap our harvest made the exhaustion of the watering and pruning feel worth it. In that moment, all of the stupid mistakes I had made in leading this group felt forgiven, or at least, forgivable. I had to ask her directly, though, what her experience with fraternal correction and restoration in this community had been. Her answer made me laugh out loud: "I think I need to think more before I speak." Before she could even finish, I interrupted, "Girl, me too!"

We talked about the sanctifying process of collaborating not just in community but also in art and the importance of apologizing, correcting, and rebuilding together. In the same way that we're learning to create art, this space has given us the opportunity to learn to create something for and within each other.

It's a little like pregnancy and labor.

It's a little like crucifixion and resurrection.

It's a little like watching the Gospel story play out in our own living room—on painted ceilings and while drinking coffee around the kitchen table.

On earth—around the piano or the easel or the pen and paper—as it is in heaven.

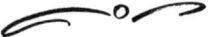

Reflection QUESTIONS

- » What do artists owe to other artists?
- » Do you have a community in which you can grow as a creative? What is your role in that community?
- » How well do you give constructive criticism? How well do you receive it?
- » Who is another artist you want to invest in, and how will you do it?

Conclusion

TELL ME ABOUT THE VIEW...

(Getting Started . . . Now)

A few years back, during an otherwise uneventful hike through Sequoia National Park, the course of my life was unexpectedly, immediately set in stone.

Well, granite, really.

As my best friend Miriam and I wandered our way through the hiking trails, pausing to lean against the trunks of the three-hundred-foot sequoia trees surrounding us, it felt as if we were weaving between the legs of giants. Underneath the canopy of green and brown and blue, I felt impossibly small and powerless—and yet also somehow that because of my smallness, I could get away with anything at all.

As it so often does, nature offered me a metaphor, drawing me a topography of my youth and artistry on the forest floor: in the shadows of the behemoths, I carried no weight and yet, in my imperceptibility, I found my freedom.

And I suppose that's how I had been living my creative life up until then. With delicate steps, never putting too much weight on either foot or committing to a singular path. I was creating as a Christian, but I wasn't creating for Christ, lest it draw too much negative attention, making me enemies and losing me work. I just danced over the roots and rocks of my life noncommittally, assuming that if the wind really wanted to blow me somewhere, it would but knowing that no matter where I landed, I wouldn't land there too hard.

After some time exploring, we stepped through the curtain of the forest brush and found ourselves at the foot of Moro Rock, a huge granite configuration that juts over the edge of the forest and looms over the park, casting a huge shadow below and offering a treacherous walkway above.

The park rangers had installed metal rails along the sides of the 350 stone steps that led brave hikers to the top of the rock if they so dared. Miriam and I exchanged our signature impish glance and nod, the one that had always given our parents pause about whether we should be spending so much time together, and headed over to begin the treacherous climb.

Right as we were about to begin, a group of elderly tourists who had just stepped off a tour bus approached us. With their beige bucket hats, bulky sneakers, and tube socks pulled up to their knees, they were a welcome sight to Miriam and me, as we both hold intergenerational friendships in the highest esteem.

"Young ladies, are you about to climb that?"

We screwed up our faces, giving our grittiest smolders: "Oh, heck yeah, we are."

We chatted for a bit and then parted ways so they could go listen to their bus driver shout out scientific and historical facts about Moro Rock. But as we turned away, one crackling voice called after us.

"Girls!"

A woman, probably around eighty years old, had stayed back from the rest of her group and was motioning for us to come back to her. We shuffled over dutifully, expecting her to say something grandmotherly about being extra careful as we climbed.

I was surprised when I saw the emotion in her eyes. She looked up at the many-stepped Moro Rock and sighed before looking back at us.

"We'll never make it up there. Me, I've got this bad hip, and the rest of them"—she paused and gave the rest of her crew an affectionate once-over—"are just plain old."

We nodded sympathetically, unsure what to say.

"I waited my whole life for these kinds of trips. I did everything right. Got married, raised kids, worked hard, and saved money, all so I could see the world someday. And now here I am, finally, and I can't even climb the darn rock and see the view."

We stayed silent, unsure of how to respond to this.

"Will you go up there for me now? And when you come back down, will you tell me about the view?"

Finally, we knew what to say. Yes, of course we would come back and tell her all about it—how the key-like ridges of the mountain ranges seemed to unlock the sky, how the birds looked more like they were swimming than flying, and how everything looking smaller below you doesn't actually make you feel any bigger.

When we got back down from climbing the ledge though, the bus was gone and, with it, our friend.

Rolling Away the Stone

I was surprised at how moved I was by that brief encounter. And that movement wasn't just a brief breeze through my sympathies or an exercise in understanding my own mortality but rather something more solid, like a stone getting dislodged within me.

Through that conversation, some sort of airway within me cleared, allowing the breath of the Holy Spirit to move more freely through my chest, giving new oxygen to my mind and exhalation to my mouth. I suddenly understood that my light-footed dancing through the forest wasn't how I wanted to move through life or my artistry at all. I didn't want to waltz through life, no! I wanted to take big, bold, risky skips down an intentional path, unflinching as the pebbles and dust rolled under my feet and the branches gave way beneath the weight of who I was being called to become.

This transition called to mind a prayer written by St. John Henry Newman, often referred to as "Some Definite Service." One section in particular struck me:

> God knows me and calls me by my name....
> God has created me to do Him some definite service;
> He has committed some work to me
> which He has not committed to another.
> I have my mission—I never may know it in this life,
> but I shall be told it in the next.
> Somehow I am necessary for His purposes...
> I have a part in this great work;
> I am a link in a chain, a bond of connection
> between persons.
> He has not created me for naught. I shall do good,

> I shall do His work;
> I shall be an angel of peace, a preacher of truth."[1]

I hope this book has given you a bit of the creative courage that I so often lack. I'd like to think that the simple act of writing it has made me braver too—as an artist and a believer.

In the moments when my courage has faltered or laziness and fear have overcome me, Newman's words have pulled me up off the floor and back to my writing desk: "He knows what He is about."

So often, I forget what I'm about. Am I an intrepid artist? Am I a steadfast Christian? Am I daring or am I devoted? Can I be both?

When I lose sight of who I am or what he has called me to create, I need only look at the reflections of him all around me to once again be washed in his certainty. I find those reflections most brilliant not in the art around me but in the *artists* around me—artists like you.

Thank you in advance for what you will create: the songs and poems you will write, the canvases you will paint, and the films you will craft. There's no way of knowing how many people will meet him through you and your work, but I know they will.

He knows what he is about—and if you create for him—others will too.

Appendix

YOUR
"ARTIST DATES"

So, now what? You've read my stories; read wisdom on beauty, truth, and goodness from great saints, authors, and popes; and even taken some time and space to answer questions on how all of this can apply to you and your life. But how can you take all of this and apply it to your real life?

Let me start by saying, not everyone has to start a Catholic artist colony, even if it sure would be cool if you did. And as I wrote at the beginning of this book, profiting from your art isn't what defines you as an artist either, so please don't feel you have to go out and immediately begin publishing stories or selling your paintings in order to prove that you got something valuable from this book.

Instead, I have assembled nine "artist dates" that you can spend with a trusted friend or fellow creative to map out what might be next for you each as a creative. Each date reflects one of the chapters and the lessons it holds. I hope this will serve as a practical tool for you to apply these stories and lessons to your own practice!

Artist Date!
A PLACE TO CALL HOME

What would it look like for you to start a renaissance of artists in your own hometown, college town, or the city you settled in after school? How would you cultivate community and creativity not just in yourself but also in others?

On a practical level, how might you attract those other artists if you haven't found them already? In my experience, having public performances and art-sharing opportunities always attracts those with a shared interest in beauty, truth, and goodness. It might also be worthwhile to remain open to collaborating with the people you'll meet through this who don't always share your exact background or belief system. You'll be surprised at the way beauty can break down barriers between different types of people since it calls us to something higher than ourselves.

Most cities provide funding and grants for public art-making. Check out the website of the mayor's office of your city for cultural and arts grants that you can apply for to bring beauty to your neighborhood. Similarly, you'd be surprised how many apostolates and church initiatives are looking to partner with creatives as they seek innovative ways to bring the Gospel to young people and marginalized communities. Summon your courage and reach out to organizations, brands, and individuals who align with your values and ask to collaborate creatively!

Date Idea: Plan an event or meetups for creatives in your area.

Artist Date 2
WHAT MAKES AN ARTIST?

By now you've read quite a bit about what does and doesn't make an artist. But reading something once doesn't mean you've internalized it. As corny as it may sound, consider leaving affirmations of your identity around the space that you live and create in. These can be simple reminders of the beauty you're able to create or even quotes from artists you admire or Bible verses on your prolific nature.

I'd also suggest that it's easier to remember that you're an artist and refer to yourself aloud as an artist when you're constantly creating. Set small goals for yourself: Write one or two lines a day, sketch one picture a day, or sing one song a day—anything you have to do to maintain consistency.

Confidence is the result of a million small promises kept to ourselves, so if you can keep the small promise of creating just a little bit every day, you will build your confidence as a creative.

Similarly, taking the time to reach out and affirm other artists whose work you admire will in turn build your confidence. When we're feeling low or insecure, there can be a temptation to retreat into self-pity. Rather, I would suggest ignoring that instinct and instead reaching *outwardly* to affirm others' work. You'll be surprised at how this heals your relationship with creating and creators.

Date Idea: Get coffee together and write letters of gratitude and affirmation to an artist whose work you admire. If possible, send the letter.

Artist Date 3
HOW TO MAKE IT LOOK AS IF YOU'RE HAVING FUN DANCING

If my advice in the first chapter tells you *how* to attract and build a creative community, then my advice in chapter 3 is on how to curate that community to make sure you are being uplifted just as often as you are the one doing the uplifting.

First, I suggest taking the title of the chapter quite literally. I truly believe that if you want to become a more honest artist, you should go out with your friends and practice ego abandonment on the dance floor. It is such a fun and low-risk way to learn to step outside of yourself and the cage of others' perceptions of you and your self-expression.

Second, add a little levity to your art-making practice in general. It shouldn't always be so serious. I know the trend is to paint ourselves as starving and tortured artists, but that exists in tension with our identity as joy-filled children of God. Allow yourself to create, just as you might dance, just for fun.

Date Idea: Invite your partner to go dancing. Then come home early and create about it.

Artist Date 4
FEED THE HUNGER INSIDE YOU

This chapter came with quite a bit of prescriptive advice already and is perhaps the most straightforward. Go into nature. Walk around your city without headphones on. Go to Confession, receive the Eucharist, and then sit on the grass with your bare feet folded beneath you and create something lovely.

Sometimes it can take a little while to adjust to these lifestyle changes and let them take effect on your mind and soul. My advice is to set a goal for how long you want to try them before making up your mind on whether they add to your life.

Date Idea: Find an accountability buddy and agree to one week without headphones. At the end of the week, meet up for Confession and Mass and then discuss how the increased sensitivity affected your art-making.

Artist Date 5
MAKING SPACE

This chapter can be daunting! It's a call to throw away a lot of the attachments that may be holding you back as a creator—physically, socially, emotionally, and spiritually. And what type of person would ever want to do all that? Give up all of your comforts just for the possibility of creating something beautiful, true, and good? Well, friend, I'm betting that *you* might be that type of person.

Below, I've created a table to help you sort through some of the areas in your life that might need a little clearing out. The idea isn't to just throw everything out—a lot of these aspects of your life can be reordered and redeemed in a way that can serve you in this new chapter.

For this artist date, fill out the table and then bring it to a trusted advisor—someone who is at least five years ahead of you on this journey—and discuss what you learned about where you've been, and where you're going.

Appendix: Your "Artist Dates"

	DO I FEEL THAT I CURRENTLY HAVE THIS KIND OF SPACE IN ABUNDANCE?	WHAT IS MAKING THIS PART OF MY LIFE FEEL CROWDED? WHAT ISN'T SERVING ME?	HOW CAN I REDEEM THE PARTS OF MY LIFE THAT FEEL CROWDED? CAN I LEARN TO CREATE FROM THE SPACES THAT USED TO MAKE ME FEEL SUFFOCATED?
PHYSICAL SPACE			
SOCIAL SPACE			
EMOTIONAL SPACE			
SPIRITUAL SPACE			

Artist Date 6

SUCCESS IS THE BEST REVENGE

If a million small failures build resiliency, then a million small victories build confidence and strength. Set small goals as you build both your belief in yourself and your overall practice. These will restore you.

Write out one small goal to accomplish by the end of each week for the next month. Make them manageable so you know you're setting yourself up for success. While it may be scary, my best advice is to be extremely open with others about your goals as a means of accountability.

As I also mentioned in this chapter, consider extending grace to those who you feel have hindered or mocked your creative journey. You'd be shocked at the type of pain and shame those individuals are often carrying about their own artistic work and path.

Date Idea: At the end of four weeks of promises kept to yourself, meet up with your accountability partner and CELEBRATE!

Artist Date 7
CREATE WITH YOUR CROSS

A friend once received an assignment from her writing professor to write the one story they knew they weren't allowed to write.

At first, she told me that she just shrugged, knowing she was an adult who could write about anything she wanted. But after a bit more reflection, she realized there was a story that she had been holding in, something she felt was too painful and personal to write about.

Consider what in your life might be deserving of restoration through creation. What crosses can be used as paintbrush and pen? Might art-making serve a healing purpose in your life? Give yourself permission to tell those stories, if only for your personal catharsis and prayer life.

As I mentioned in this chapter, be intentional about whom you share these very personal projects with.

Date Idea: Process a long-held pain through art-making. If you do not have a safe place or person to bring that project, consider bringing it to a trusted priest through Confession.

Artist Date 8
LABOR TOWARD NEW LIFE

I'm sure that this chapter reads differently for women than it does for men. And I'm sure it reads even more differently for women who have been pregnant and birthed children than it does for women like myself who have not. However, I believe everyone can gain something from understanding their creative process through this lens.

On a practical note, I would suggest that you identify which stage of the process you and your creative practice are in right now: romance, conception, gestation, labor, or the holding of the creation against your beating heart. Knowing where you stand allows you to know what to do next.

There is a slowness to both physical and creative pregnancy, and I would encourage you to glory in that slowness instead of resenting it, as I have often made the mistake of doing. If it all happened quickly, the way you may want it, you wouldn't be prepared. Even further, if it didn't hurt so much and cost so much, you'd probably never understand what your creation is worth. Thank God for the fortitude he has given you to carry your creation into this world.

Date Idea: Draw the gestation stages of your art-making. Don't be afraid to make this a visual art project.

Artist Date 9
THEATER KIDS WILL INHERIT THE WORLD

Where in your creative practice, as an individual or as a community, do you need restoration? As I shared in this chapter, I received creative restoration from the investment that Shannon made in me. Similarly, I received a different sort of peace and restoration from investing in our artist in residence, Molly. Is there someone in whom you can invest some of your creativity and time to restore old wounds about your creative practice?

On the flip side, consider writing down what type of artist you would like to be someday. Use descriptive qualities about not only the skills and experiences you'd like to have but also the person you'd like to be. Look at that list and try to think of someone, maybe five to ten years ahead of you, who could possibly serve as a mentor to you.

Date Idea: Reach out to someone whom you would love to learn from, and ask them if you can pick their brain over coffee.

Notes

2. What Makes an Artist?
1. G. K. Chesterton, *Chesterton's Orthodoxy: Countering Contemporary Philosophies* (Delhi: Grapevine India, 2023), 30–31.
2. John Paul II, "Letter to Artists," April 4, 1999, https://www.vatican.va/content/john-paul-ii/en/letters/1999/documents/hf_jp-ii_let_23041999_artists.html.

3. How to Make It Look as if You're Having Fun Dancing
1. C. S. Lewis, *The Four Loves* (New York: Harper One, 1960), 83.
2. Eric Weiner, "Where Heaven and Earth Come Closer," *New York Times*, March 9, 2012.

4. Feed the Hunger Inside You
1. Joseph Ratzinger, "The Feeling of Things, the Contemplation of Beauty," August 24, 2002, https://www.vatican.va/roman_curia/congregations/cfaith/documents/rc_con_cfaith_doc_20020824_ratzinger-cl-rimini_en.html.
2. Ratzinger, "The Feeling of Things."

8. Labor toward New Life
1. John Paul II, "Letter to Artists," 5.
2. Henri J. M. Nouwen, *Clowning in Rome: Reflections on Solitude, Celibacy, Prayer, and Contemplation* (Garden City, NY: Image Books, 1979), 83–84.
3. John Paul II, *God Is Beauty* (Theology of the Body Institute Press, 2021), 33–34.
4. John Paul II, *God Is Beauty*, 34.

Conclusion
1. John Henry Newman, "Meditations on Christian Doctrine: Hope in God—Creator," in *Meditations and Devotions*, edited by W. P. Neville (New York: Longmans, Green, and Co., 1907), 299.

Clare McCallan founded and serves as the creative director at St. Joseph's Home for Artisans and is a touring spoken-word poet. She is the creator and host of *The Renaissance Room* and cohost of *This Is the Day* on CatholicTV, where she also works as a writer.

McCallan earned a bachelor's degree at Franciscan University of Steubenville. She contributes to NBC10's *The Hub Today*, the Christian Channel, *National Catholic Reporter*, FemCatholic, and the Grotto Network. She is the host of the *Letters from the Least* podcast.

She has been featured on numerous television shows and podcasts.

claremmccallan@gmail.com
Facebook: Clare McCallan
Instagram: @clare_mccallan

Valerie Delgado is a Catholic painter, a digital artist, and the owner of Pax.Beloved. She illustrated the books *Prepare Your Heart* and *Made for Heaven* by Fr. Agustino Torres, CFR; *Adore* by Fr. John Burns; *Restore* by Sr. Miriam James Heidland, SOLT; and *ABC Get to Know the Saints with Me* by Caroline Perkins.

She lives in the Houston, Texas, area.

www.paxbeloved.com
Instagram: @pax.valerie

Ave Maria Press

Founded in 1865, Ave Maria Press, a ministry of the Congregation of Holy Cross, is a Catholic publishing company that serves the spiritual and formative needs of the Church and its schools, institutions, and ministers; Christian individuals and families; and others seeking spiritual nourishment.

For a complete listing of titles from

Ave Maria Press

Sorin Books

Forest of Peace

Christian Classics

visit www.avemariapress.com